THE
SNOWY
CABIN
COOKBOOK

ALSO BY MARNIE HANEL AND JEN STEVENSON

The Picnic (coauthors)
The Campout Cookbook
Summer: A Cookbook

THE
SNOWY
CABIN
COOKBOOK

**MEALS AND DRINKS FOR ADVENTUROUS DAYS
AND COZY NIGHTS**

MARNIE HANEL & JEN STEVENSON
ILLUSTRATIONS BY MONICA DORAZEWSKI

ARTISAN | NEW YORK

Library of Congress Cataloging-in-Publication Data

Names: Hanel, Marnie, author. | Stevenson, Jen, 1977– author. |
Dorazewski, Monica, illustrator.
Title: The snowy cabin cookbook : meals and drinks for adventurous days
and cozy nights / Marnie Hanel & Jen Stevenson ; illustrations by Monica
Dorazewski.
Description: New York : Artisan, a division of Workman Publishing Co., Inc.
[2021] | Includes index.
Identifiers: LCCN 2021004794 | ISBN 9781579659455 (hardcover)
Subjects: LCSH: Seasonal cooking. | Winter—Miscellanea. | Cookbooks. lcgft
Classification: LCC TX714 .H3616 2021 | DDC 641.5/64—dc23
LC record available at https://lccn.loc.gov/2021004794

Design by Renata De Oliveira

Artisan books are available at special discounts when purchased in bulk for
premiums and sales promotions as well as for fund-raising or educational
use. Special editions or book excerpts also can be created to specification. For
details, contact the Special Sales Director at the address below, or send an
e-mail to specialmarkets@workman.com.

For speaking engagements, contact speakersbureau@workman.com.

Published by Artisan
A division of Workman Publishing Co., Inc., 225 Varick Street,
New York, NY 10014-4381
artisanbooks.com

Artisan is a registered trademark of Workman Publishing Co., Inc.

Published simultaneously in Canada by Thomas Allen & Son, Limited

Printed in China

First printing, September 2021

10 9 8 7 6 5 4 3 2 1

for the
SNOWDRIFT
SET

Contents

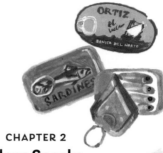

Preface

Peeking out the window to see a world quieted by freshly fallen snow is a matchless joy, promising a day filled with wintry adventures bookended by warm, nourishing meals. As brisk weather slows our daily pace, we find more reasons to gather and time to cook, because as much as we love skiing, sledding, skating, snowshoeing, and snowball fighting, ultimately, when the wind is whipping up outside, we take a shine to being inside. Braving the chill makes the chili/braise/no-holds-barred cabin bar feel like just deserts—and speaking of desserts, any season all about enjoying them is A-OK with us. (If that's you, too, turn directly to chapter 5.)

We hope you'll use this book as a guide to creating holiday-level happiness on any given day, whether as a primer for a party or a planner for a week filled with Alpine-inspired activities, which could take place in a snowy cabin, a ski house rental, an Alsatian chalet (our personal sugarplum dream), or your own festive home. You'll find in this book a surfeit of fireside snacks, suppers that—whether because they come together easily or are even better warmed up the next day—keep you in the conversation and not just the kitchen, delicious desserts, bountiful booze, and beautiful breakfasts. There's enough chocolate and cheese in here to transport you to a Swiss mountaintop, but if that's not your fantasy destination, the menus throughout the book can whisk you to any number of idyllic escapes. Many of the projects in these pages, such as Perfect Your Raclette Etiquette (page 110) and our dumpling deep dive (see pages 116–119), are essentially group activities that end in a meal.

You'll also find ways to cook for a delightful date, provision a snowshoe picnic, and ace feeding a hungry family in the poorly equipped kitchen of a faraway dwelling.

With an eye to that getaway-cabin scenario, before you hit the road, check the packing lists of essential equipment that follow the recipes you're planning to make. That way you won't leave home without your Microplane grater (which is probably a principle to live by) or can anticipate what you might need to improvise/compromise. Given that you might be stocking a bar for a weekend, not a lifetime, we aimed for a broad cocktail list intended to offer options to explore a new interest. Whether you're a mezcal maven or a Scotch savant, we suggest that you pick a snowy lane (in the form of a good bottle) and stick with it. When it comes to pantry ingredients, look to the bulk bins to buy small quantities so you'll have the freshest spices while you're on the road—particularly for those gingerbread spices you're less likely to use year-round. (Note: All recipes were developed using Diamond Crystal kosher salt.)

This is the season of dinners with friends, game nights with family, baking projects, and a pot of soup perpetually warming on the stovetop to feed anyone who wanders out of their book nook looking for lunch. Whether you're planning for yourself, a pair, or a crowd; whether you're a beginner or an experienced cook; whether you're just here for the fondue or the stocking stuffer (the book fits—we checked); we hope you'll find something that delights you in these pages.

Now let's hope for a snow day! And be sure to show off your delicacies as you do. Join us online at #snowycabincookbook to share your sundries, see photos that inspired the beautiful illustrations by Monica Dorazewski, and pop by with any questions for a virtual fireside chat. In the season in which everyone gravitates to the kitchen, we couldn't be happier to have you in ours.

xo,
Marnie and Jen

CHAPTER 1

From Snowshoes to Slippers

When contemplating your snow-day foray, certain frigid-weather fundamentals must be taken into account while planning and packing, lest you accidentally barrel into the backcountry sans striped retro ski suits, schnitzel fixings, or the shotski (see page 172). This concise cabin compendium will guide you from home to lodge hearth, helping to ensure that the family snowmobile is properly outfitted with tire chains and emergency road snacks, every mitten has a match and every leaky snow tube a patch, no fewer than a dozen cabin fever relievers are at the ready should blizzard-induced boredom set in, and the slow cooker and schnapps are firmly stowed somewhere between the snowboard boots and the après-ski Snuggies.

Cabin Compendium

Much like a handful of snow down the back of your coat collar, forgetting something vital on a snow play getaway—be it boots, bourbon, or to buy firewood—is a dire and dismaying surprise. Stick close to these cold-weather canons, and rest assured that you'll never be bereft of tire chains (or tasty snacks to eat while watching someone else put them on), craving chili con carne sans a slow cooker, gazing gloomily at a cold and empty fireplace, or up Beaver Creek without a radler.

Fleece Release

Assuming you did in fact pack it away last spring, it's time to haul your winter wardrobe up from the basement, down from the attic, or out of the oven (you'll need the oven space for Chalet Cassoulet, page 136, anyway). This is the time for those warm woolly sweaters, luscious layers of fleece, faux fur–trimmed waterproof boots, and mismatched mittens to shine. It's also a good opportunity to check that your gear's in order: every ski and pole needs a partner, every helmet needs a pair of good-fitting goggles, and every pair of ice skates needs a pair of padded undershorts.

Snowmobile Sensibilities

Before setting your sleigh's GPS to Timberline or Telluride, be sure it's road ready: check the tire treads and pressure; make sure the wiper blades and battery are in mint condition; pack the jumper cables, tire chains, snow scraper, and a compact folding snow shovel; and compile an emergency kit with food, water, a first-aid kit, flashlights, flares, blankets, and a bag of sand or cat litter to provide traction for particularly serious stuck-wheel situations (cat optional, but cozy).

Meal Plan

If traveling with cold-weather cohorts, before you begin packing, start a shared online spreadsheet for menu planning and cooking assignments. Determine who's in charge of each fireside feast (and the resulting dish duty), what ingredients and equipment are needed, and, perhaps paramount, who has bar duty, because those calvados cocktails aren't going to mix themselves. Keep a tally of expenses, and settle up via Venmo.

Cabin Crew

Goggles and gloves are helpful—some might say mandatory—when on a mountain mini break, but hell hath no fury like a famished group of melted-cheese-obsessed rippers and shredders who've just been informed that the cabin has no raclette grill. If your kitchen is operating with a skeleton crew, equipment-wise, think about adding a few helping hands— a slow cooker, cast-iron skillet, sharp chef's knife, and wine opener—as well as a few fun extra-credit add-ons: the aforementioned raclette grill, a fondue set, and an electric skillet (for panfrying dozens of dumplings at once; see page 119). Not to mention a Flexible Flyer for schlepping everything.

Boot Brigade

As snow bunnies return to home base and snow pants and ski poles start to fly, all sense of cabin order can quickly become buried under a pile of soggy wool socks. Establish a faux foyer if there isn't a real one, leaving snowy boots by the door and keeping equipment neatly corralled. Check the laundry room for a lightweight folding drying rack or two to create extra space for hanging wet bibs, beanies, snow picnic blankets, and swimsuits (should your chalet have a hot tub).

Contingency Cans

Fresh powder and power lines don't always get along, so be sure you've got a backup plan should a whiteout be on the way. Stockpile firewood and flashlights; keep snacks and ready-to-warm soups on hand; stow a few gallons (12 L) of drinking water per person; buy a supply of instant coffee, tea, and tipples; and remember that cornmeal pancakes taste all the more delicious when flipped in a cast-iron skillet heated atop the potbelly stove.

Hygge How-To

In Denmark and Norway, where the winters are cold and dark, the art of creating a deliciously cozy refuge is called hygge (*hue-gah*), the basic goal of which is making every room feel like the place you'd most want to take a nap. It's been a few years since we first discovered there was a word for our favorite feeling, and now we've pretty much perfected it. Apply the practice by stocking these homey essentials.

Wood-Burning Fireplace
Aka the heart of the hygge.

Just a Smudge
Light a little sage or palo santo to clear the cabin's energy and raclette aroma.

Shearling Slippers
Because it's ughs vs. Uggs.

Trivial Pursuits
Pick your pleasure: puzzles, games, yarn-related crafts, punch-needle embroidery.

Scented Candles

Vanilla, tobacco, sandalwood >
ski boots, fondue, bunk room.

Throw Blankets

Drape 'em by the dozen.

Flannel Sheets

Herein, hospitable hibernation.

Electric Kettle

Keep the hot drinks flowing.

Hot-Water Bottle

Tuck one into each bed when it's
time for a nightcap.

Whiskey Bar

Fully stocked with our favorite mixer:
no judgment.

Scout Your Slope

Poring over French chalet profile pictures to find just the right plunge pool and wraparound terrace, filtering through word-of-mouth recommendations for the most fetching log A-frame on the Roaring Fork River, watching igloo-building how-to videos on YouTube—it's hard work hunting for the perfect snow shelter, but all that legwork will be well worth it when you're sipping post-slope hot whiskey ciders by a crackling fire as the Northern Lights flicker overhead.

Topography

- ☐ Gentle, snowy, tree-speckled slope positioned squarely beneath an aurora
- ☐ Devoid of raccoon, cougar, wolf, and wolverine dens
- ☐ A safe distance from the beginning, middle, or end of an avalanche zone
- ☐ Near or in a small town that looks like it came straight out of a Hallmark holiday movie
- ☐ Scenic mountain meadow, Mariah Carey's Christmas tree, or Olympic super-G finish line views

Amenities

- ☐ Wood-burning fireplace
- ☐ Wood
- ☐ Snow-veiled back porch hot tub
- ☐ Twelve-person cedar sauna
- ☐ Walking distance to the Million Dollar Cowboy Bar

Not Within 100 Feet of Site

- ☐ Snowplow storage yard
- ☐ Large, energetic groups of snowmobile racers
- ☐ Polar bear burrow
- ☐ Biathlon firing range
- ☐ Annie Wilkes's house

If you've checked all the boxes, congratulations—you're ready to cozy up in comfort!

At Which Chalet Will You Stay?

Whether you're planning on going five-star in the Swiss Alps or pitching a snow tent, this simple, straightforward yes-or-no decision tree will help you find just the right spot to hang your beanie at the end of a long and satisfying snow day.

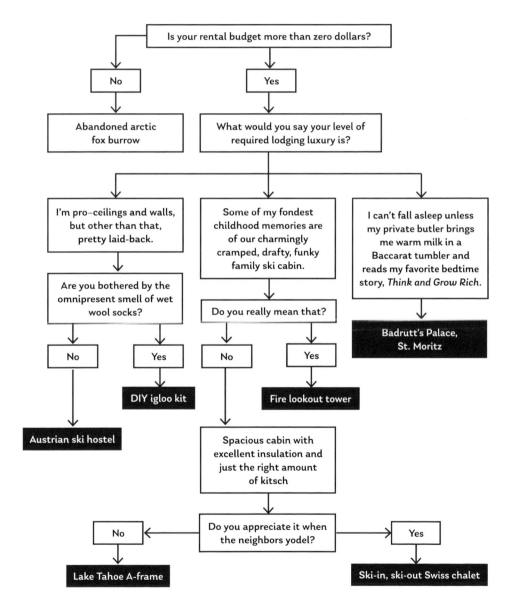

Hooray! You've found your home sleet home!

Watch Sparks Fly

When the weather outside is frightful, a fire is so delightful—except if you're dashing around, frantically flinging open doors and windows, and fanning out smoke, because you forgot to open the damper. Before you throw in the kitchen towel,* consult this guide to setting up a cozy, flickering fire, which is the heart of cabin life and absolutely essential, no matter how much drama it takes to get there.

Hearth Housekeeping

Cozy up to the fireplace in seven foolproof steps.

1. Gather dry logs, kindling (small sticks the width of candy canes), and tinder (twigs, newspaper twists, fire starters).

2. Sweep the hearth of excess ash (greater than a 1-inch/2.5 cm depth) and cart it away in a metal pail.

3. Open the damper.

4. Double-check that you opened the damper.

5. Did you really open the damper?

6. Prime the flue to guard against the possibility of a smoke-filled living room by either waiting 30 minutes for ambient room air to displace cold air or lighting a roll of newspaper and holding it up the chimney to warm things up.

7. Now lay the fire. While there are many A+ methods for doing so, we're all for the way that allows the fire to self-feed while you sit back with your boots up. It's called an upside-down fire, and here's how you build it: Set two logs in a parallel position (on the log holder, if there is one), top with two more logs in the opposite parallel position (aka Lincoln Log–style), top those with a layer of kindling, and finish with a layer of tinder. Light from the top and sit back to admire your homey handiwork.

Song of Ice and Fire

Neither snow nor sleet should keep you from s'mores outdoors. Set up a bonfire like so.

1. Scout a spot that's protected from the wind and features no low-hanging, snow-laden branches above.

2. Find a large, flat rock to use as the fire floor, or build a platform of wood, rocks, or a sheet pan.

3. Lay the fire as instructed in step 7 of Hearth Housekeeping.

4. Set logs around the fire for seating, and gather the other s'mores essentials: roasting sticks, marshmallows, graham crackers, and chocolate—and wet wipes (just kidding, but not kidding).

*Please don't; it's a fire hazard.

A Word on Woodstoves

Decode the mysteries of the cabin's sole heat source in seven steps.

1. When faced with an unfamiliar woodstove, the first step is to figure out how to maximize airflow. Open the air intake with the lever located under or beside the door. Next, open the damper above the firebox that controls the flue.

2. Pile tinder inside the firebox and top with kindling. Light a small fire, keeping the door open until the kindling lights, then add more kindling and close the door, without latching it.

3. Once the fire is established, add a log and close and latch the door. Wait about 10 minutes, until the log is burning, open the door slowly (to avoid introducing a gust of air into the burn box and having to start over), and add a few logs. Relatch the door.

4. Once the logs catch, close the damper two-thirds of the way. The goal is to let enough air into the woodstove to allow the logs to burn down to hot coals, but not so much that all the warmth goes right up the chimney rather than into the cabin.

5. When only coals remain, use your fire tools to rake the coals toward the front of the stove, add more wood, and close the damper three-quarters of the way. If you're going to sleep, or leaving the cabin, close the damper most of the way, but never entirely.

6. In the morning, or every 24 hours, shovel the ashes from the firebox into a metal bucket to prevent a buildup of more than 1 inch (2.5 cm) of ash.

7. Accept all compliments from cabinmates; you're practically a pioneer.

Come on Baby, Light My Fire

Whether you're an off-the-cuff cabinmate rummaging through the cupboards for creative kindling, or a plan-ahead partyer looking for DIY starters to store fireside, with the help of this guide, you'll never again find yourself flameless.

Citrus Bundles
When you're flying through satsumas in peak citrus season, dry the peels on a plate for 3 days (or in a 200°F/95°C oven for 30 minutes). Roll tightly in a sheet of newspaper and bind with twine.

Various and Sundry Household Items
Raid the laundry room for dryer lint, the bathroom for cotton balls, and your home office for shredded mail, then stuff them into the compartments of a cardboard egg carton to tear off and use as needed.

Wax-Dipped Pinecones
Use tongs to dip dried pinecones in melted paraffin wax. Set on a wire rack to harden. Or, to cue up eye-catching white flames, sprinkle the hot wax with Epsom salts before cooling.

Fatwood
Pick up a box of this resin-rich, chemical-free sustainable kindling that's harvested from the stumps of pine trees. Just a few sticks will start a fire and leave behind little ash.

Good Herbs
Gather bunches of lavender, sage, rosemary, and thyme before the first frost. Bind with twine and hang to dry.

Potato Chips
When all else fails, sacrifice snacks to a higher purpose. Any greasy chip will do.

Ski Slang

When ski lingo and après-ski lingo cross paths and you need a translator to sort out exactly what everyone's talking about, consult this handy glossary.

Balaclava (*noun*). Snug knit cap that covers the head and neck.
vs.
Baklava (*noun*). Greek feast's grace note.

Crust (*noun*). Crunchy top layer of snow.
vs.
Crust (*noun*). Best bit of the Root Vegetable, Red Chard, Rosemary, and Rye Galette (page 112).

Death cookies (*noun*). Dangerous chunks of ice created by snowmakers and snow groomers.
vs.
Cookies (*noun*). Dangerous chunks of butter, sugar, and flour created by snow-angel makers.

French fries and pizza (*nouns*). Go-to moves on the bunny hill.
vs.
French fries and pizza (*nouns*). Items we shouldn't have ordered at two a.m.

Hot dog (*noun*). Show-off snowboarder catching big air in the park.
vs.
Hot dog (*noun*). Lunch.

Jerry (*noun*). Inexperienced skier with a gobsmacking inner guide.
vs.
Jerry (*noun*). Beloved Vermont ice cream maker; *usage* "Ben &."

Lunch tray (*noun*). Snowboard; *sounds like* "launch tray."
vs.
Lunch tray (*noun*). Viable sled alternative.

Powpow (*noun*). Freshly fallen snow.
vs.
Powpow (*noun*). Sound made fighting for the last bite of Caffè Corretto Mousse (page 149).

Shred (*verb*). To ski or snowboard with passion and proficiency.
vs.
Shred (*verb*). To follow the instructions regarding the mozzarella.

Six-pack (*noun*). Fully loaded six-person chairlift.
vs.
Six-pack (*noun*). Fully loaded craft brew carton.

Tips and Tricks: Tools

Pack these prudent portables to cook, snack, and quaff in cozy cabin comfort.

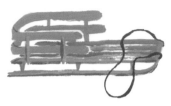

No-Horse Open Sleigh
To speed up *and* stylize car-to-cabin schlepping.

Knife and Cutting Board
For slicing and dicing hot-pot heatables.

Cheese Slicer
Because there will be raclette, and lots of it.

Thermos
Stow slopeside sips, be they of the hot chocolate or hot-toddy variety.

Fireplace Popcorn Popper
When ambience transcends efficiency.

Electric Kettle
For those immediate mint tea, spiced cider mix, and instant noodle cup needs.

Bar Tool Travel Kit
Never leave home without a shaker, strainer, jigger, and muddler again.

Rimmed Sheet Pan
One-pan supper hero; doubles as a snow saucer in a pinch.

Slow Cooker
A luscious roast goes in, you go out— dinner prep: done.

Cast-Iron Skillet
For makin' bacon, pan pizza, and big burly brownie sundaes.

Fondue Set
Melt cheese, chocolate, and melted-cheese-and-chocolate-loving hearts.

Shabu-Shabu Pot
Neatly divided for those who like it spicy hot and those who do not.

99 Ways (and Counting) to Use a Mug

1. Snowflake catcher
2. Hand warmer
3. Super-sturdy soup bowl
4. Hot-toddy holder
5. Recipe card roost
6. Eggnog enclosure
7. Hockey puck pocket
8. Reindeer feeder
9. Snowperson prop
10. Gingerbread-man man cave
11. Snowball safekeeper
12. Candleholder
13. Candy cane cask
14. Slow snow shovel
15. Inspirational quote billboard
16. Hot cocoa corral
17. Irish coffee concealer
18. Stocking stuffer
19. Biscuit cutter
20. Winter wineglass
21. Cramped Christmas cookie jar
22. Cabin doorstop
23. Ripe pear protector
24. Ice-fishing hole tracer
25. Egg poacher
26. Sugarplum storage
27. Microwave cake maker
28. Soufflé baker
29. Dinner table placeholder
30. Icicle knocker-offer
31. Jell-O mold
32. Twinkle-light detangler
33. Pinecone pedestal
34. Popcorn portioner
35. Stew server
36. Boot stretcher
37. Boot lift
38. Rib roast rub receptacle
39. Quintessential hoardable
40. Mosaic material
41. Pint-size firepit
42. Quaint cabin kitsch
43. Poinsettia planter
44. Opaque parfait pot
45. Spider catch-and-releaser
46. Wee winter herb garden

47. Chili cauldron
48. Sleigh valet tip jar
49. Circle stamper
50. Pretzel mix pail
51. Toboggan parking block
52. Itty-bitty ice rink
53. Sled dog kibble dipper
54. Leaky roof lifesaver
55. Ice skate sharpener
56. Unstable umbrella bucket
57. Nonglamorous party swag
58. Jumbo ice cube mold
59. Hail measurer
60. Chowder chamber
61. Mug tree hanger-on
62. Elf step stool
63. Uncomfortable earmuff
64. Punch glass
65. Peppermint ice cream scooper
66. Kindling keeper
67. Spare-change jar
68. Tinsel trapper
69. Impromptu gift box
70. Penguin foot bath
71. Clunky Christmas ornament
72. Sugar packet pod
73. Holly sprig holder
74. Conspicuous flask
75. Paper clip coop

76. Ribbon spool
77. Mitten trap
78. Soap dish
79. Petite planter box
80. New Year's Eve noisemaker
81. Knitting needle nook
82. Escaped fireplace coal catcher
83. Desk organizer
84. Mulled cider stein
85. Chickadee sanctuary
86. Flour fetcher
87. iPhone amplifier
88. Sponge stander-upper
89. Crude cruet
90. Gravy boat
91. Nonsecure safe
92. Measuring cup
93. Dolcetto decanter
94. Tiny trash bin
95. Ski trip souvenir
96. Beer fund bank
97. White elephant gift
98. Pre-mistletoe-kiss breath tester
99. Barbie Dream Chalet hot tub

Reindeer Games: Cabin Fever Relievers

These fun alfresco activities will upgrade your usual reindeer games ("find the car keys we dropped in the snow" and "sprint from the front door to the recycling bin holding two bags of empty mulled wine bottles") while raising vitamin D levels, heart rates, and cabin-fever-depleted sanity levels.

Tic-Tac-Snow

Stomp out an extra-large 3-by-3-square tic-tac-toe grid in fresh powder, then commence playing with snow saucers for Os and crossed skis or poles for Xs. If snow saucer and ski pole inventory is low, draw a smaller grid and employ good old pinecones and twigs.

Dress the Snowperson

Take turns blindfolding players and laughing uncontrollably as they try to correctly position a carrot nose, stick mouth, pair of sunglasses, hat, scarf, and swimsuit on a premade snowperson. Extra credit to everyone if the owner of the swimsuit comes home in the middle of the game.

Snowlympics

Set up your own version of the Winter Games: use a snowball in place of the torch and relay race around the yard; hold a "bobsled" race using nonregulation bobsleds (e.g., unicorn snow tubes, boogie boards, chaise lounge cushions); and tamp down a long flat stretch of snow, then use Frisbees and brooms to create a lo-fi curling competition.

Fox and Geese

In a meadow or field of freshly fallen snow, stomp out a large circle divided into eight wedges (it should look like a scrumptious snow pie). In the center, stomp out a roomy "nest," aka the safety zone. Starting in the safety zone, all players scatter, staying strictly within the pre-stomped paths (go out of bounds, and you're instantly the fox). The "fox" takes up the chase, until nabbing a hapless "goose," who then becomes the fox. Keep playing until everyone's boots have filled with snow, or until sunset, whichever comes first.

Not Hot Potato

Arrange everyone in a circle, mittens on, and pass around a potato-size chunk of ice while playing the *Cool Runnings* soundtrack. When the music stops, whoever's holding the cold potato is out. Winner gets an extra cinnamon stick in their mulled wine.

Scour the Snowscape: A Winter Scavenger Hunt

Even when the snowflakes fly, nothing escapes your eagle eye. Stroll powder-blanketed streets and slopes searching for these snow day–pertinent people, places, and things. Play until one intrepid tracker finds all twelve, or until someone appears with a tray of freshly baked Can't Catch Me Gingerbread Cakes (page 164).

	GIANT ICICLE WORTHY OF GRACING THE SET OF THE SYFY ORIGINAL MASTERPIECE *CHRISTMAS ICETASTROPHE*	
DISGRUNTLED-LOOKING SNOW SHOVELER		**CRACKED SNOW SAUCER**
	ZOMBIE SNOWPERSON	
SOMEONE STUFFING SNOW DOWN AN UNSUSPECTING VICTIM'S COLLAR	**THE ENSUING CHASE**	**YETI DEN (*EVERYONE* RUN)**

Darling, Disaster! 10 Cabin Crises Averted

When life gave you lemons, you made limoncello. And now you're going to need to drink it, because no matter how carefully you meal-planned or how considerately you packed, cabin time has hit a patch of black ice. Consult this guide to quell momentary mayhem and stay the course.

1. Ghostbusters

If you've sequestered yourself in the woods to deep-focus on a solo project only to suspect you're not alone, the first line of defense is a pencil and paper. Note every ghostly incident you encounter, be it strange noises, changes in air temperature, suspicious smells, chills down your spine, and/or objects flying around the room. With your log complete, attempt to connect the phenomena to a logical pattern, such as a passing mail truck, a drafty woodstove, burnt cookies, a prankster with an ice cube, or an enthusiastic attic bat. If no such explanation presents itself, take a seat in the murder cabin's creaky rocking chair and state your boundaries aloud (e.g., "You can turn on the old-timey television to creepy, blaring static, but *only* after eight a.m."). According to most psychics, ghosts can be pretty good listeners.

2. Shovel Off

For all the delight incited by freshly fallen snow on the ski slopes, there's an equal and opposite reaction when it's spotted on the driveway. Make the most of your unenviable winter workout by keeping the loads light (< 15 pounds/7 kg) and coating the shovel with a fine spray of WD-40 to scoop the snow and let it go.

3. Stuck in the Middle (Ear) with You

And speaking of "Let It Go," there's a good chance that if you're cooped up with a small person, your cabin time has devolved to repeat viewing of *Frozen* or a *Frozen*-adjacent film, and you're now wrestling with an earworm. To get a song out of your head, psychologist-approved tactics include chewing gum, listening to *other* earworms (seems risky), or relistening to the complete song, then immediately engaging in a cognitively absorbing task, such as mastering the Elsa braid.

4. Chill Out

When there's a draft in the cabin, a purpose-built pillow (or a lounging Bernese mountain dog) propped against the doorjamb dissuades cold air from crashing the cozy. Make your own (pillow, not puppy) on the fly by stuffing a pair of tube socks with kitchen towels and nesting the ankles to form a cylinder.

5. Frosty Reception

When there's no garage in sight, raid the kitchen cabinets to prevent ice from forming on your car overnight. Tuck the side-view mirrors inside plastic bags secured by rubber bands. Then spray the windshield with a 3:1 solution of distilled white vinegar and water for easier scraping.

6. Ah, Push It

If your car won't budge, dig out the snow around the tires and exhaust pipe, turn off the traction control, gently rock the car back and forth in a low gear, and calmly but firmly shout, "Now!" to your obliging friends.

7. Nose for Ews

When cabin air is less than fair, zap mold, mothball, or mildew odor by opening the windows for as long as you can bear it, sprinkling the carpets with baking soda and then vacuuming it up, and setting activated charcoal in the fustiest rooms. (Hopefully, not yours.)

8. Shelter in the Storm

If you're locked out with nothing but a copy of this book and a saw, build an igloo. Start by sketching the circumference by standing still and rotating a stick in a circle. Carve a door 2 feet (60 cm) lower than the rest of the structure and dig out a tunnel for the entrance. Then use a saw to carve the hard-packed snow (below the layer your feet can depress) into large rectangular blocks. Arrange the blocks in a spiral, starting with the shorter blocks and ending with the tallest. Carve and stack more blocks, making your way inward. Finish with a center block on the roof, pack the crevices on the outside with snow, and smooth the interior. Carve a vent in the ceiling, and marvel at your icy architecture.

9. Substitute Teacher

You've made the treacherous drive back from the grocery store, only to have forgotten an ingredient. Herewith, worthy substitutions.

Vanilla extract: rum

Buttermilk: 1 tablespoon lemon juice or white vinegar + enough milk to equal 1 cup (240 ml)

Cream: ¾ cup (180 ml) milk + 4 tablespoons (60 ml) melted butter

Baking powder: 1 tablespoon baking soda + 2 tablespoons cream of tartar

Fresh herbs (not for garnish): 1 teaspoon dried herbs for 1 tablespoon fresh herbs

Fondue cheese: chocolate

10. Pray for Snow

If the only thing standing in the way of you and a snow day is, well, snow, it's time to get superstitious. Pick one of these tried-and-(not-always)-true methods: sleep with your pajamas inside out and a spoon under your pillow; freeze a white crayon; put ice cubes on your porch (with a note of caution for your mail carrier); invest in a snowmaker.

Visitors' Book Bons Mots

Parting is such sweet sorrow, particularly when you're staying in a well-appointed snowy cabin that you wish could be your own but, alas, is on loan to a rotating cast of holiday revelers. After packing up, sit down and take a moment to express your gratitude in the guest book. If you're at a loss for purple prose, this Mad Libs–style template will serve as a record of your stay *and* keep future visitors intrigued.

To the host with the _____ ,
_____ _(rhyming word)_

    It was an absolute _____ to spend a weekend
                    (flattering noun)

in your _____ cabin. We were astounded by the
      (adjective)

_____ cabin decor. Was it inspired by _____ ?
(adjective)   _(film)_

We noticed you had not _____ but _____ _____
                     (number)   _(number)_   _(plural noun)_

that looked to be _____ years old. Wowza!
        (number)

    You truly thought of everything—from the _____
                                   (noun)

on our pillows to the _____ for the bathtub. Playing
                     (noun)

_____ in the _____ was a highlight. We never figured
(game)   _(room)_

out how to use the _____ , despite your _____
               (appliance)   _(adjective)_

instructions in the welcome note. We did, however, make the most of your

_____ .
(personal item)

    We should also mention we heard a _____ in/on the
                             (sound)

_____ . We assume it was a _____
(structural component of the cabin)   _(pleasant adjective)_

_____ and this will not affect our rating
(choose one: animal/fictitious woodland creature/serial killer)

on _____ .
    (booking site)

    Till next time!

_____
    (name)

The Ultimate Sleigh Soiree

Turn your one-horse open sleigh into a one-course open sleigh—pause your trusty steed in a particularly scenic snowy meadow, bundle up in a soft wool blanket or three, uncap a thermos of something belly-warming and perhaps a bit boozy, set out a sumptuous ploughman's (well, *sleighman's*) lunch, hit play on Billie Holiday's "I've Got My Love to Keep Me Warm," and watch the snowflakes fall on each other's nose, eyelashes, and Maple Walnut–Whisky Butter Tarts (page 150).

What's in Your Duffel? The Definitive Packing List

A snowy sabbatical is all the more enjoyable when you remember the aebleskiver pan, hot cocoa components, and Netflix password (because binge-watching *The Great British Baking Show* = blizzard backup plan), so heed this ambitious yet helpful list when setting up your cabin kitchen.

Essentials

- ☐ Cast-iron and nonstick skillets
- ☐ Sheet pans
- ☐ Enamelware dishes
- ☐ Cutlery
- ☐ Cooking utensils
- ☐ Aluminum foil and parchment paper
- ☐ Coffee and tea fixings
- ☐ Spices and olive oil
- ☐ Can opener
- ☐ Wine key
- ☐ Bar tools
- ☐ Microplane grater
- ☐ Box grater
- ☐ Digital thermometer
- ☐ Cutting board and knife
- ☐ Mixing bowls
- ☐ Trash and storage bags
- ☐ Paper towels and dish towels
- ☐ Dish soap and sponge
- ☐ Firewood and newspaper
- ☐ Matches or lighter
- ☐ The food!

Extras

- ☐ Trusty ol' Dutch oven
- ☐ Slow cooker
- ☐ Instant Pot
- ☐ Raclette grill
- ☐ Fondue set
- ☐ Aebleskiver pan
- ☐ Electric kettle
- ☐ Electric skillet
- ☐ Immersion blender
- ☐ High-speed blender
- ☐ Portable cocktail bar
- ☐ Champagne bucket
- ☐ S'mores sticks
- ☐ Pancake pen
- ☐ Muffin tin
- ☐ Fine-mesh sieve
- ☐ Handheld mandoline
- ☐ Citrus juicer
- ☐ Leftovers containers
- ☐ Scrabble: Cooking Edition
- ☐ Monogrammed beer steins
- ☐ Six-person shotski

STRATTON

CHAPTER 2

Slope Snacks

Any preparedness professional knows that the priority when planning the perfect winter weekend isn't lift tickets and long underwear, it's a seemingly bottomless stockpile of snacks, because nothing derails snow-spree glee like a Sausage Rolls and Sambal-Spiced Wings shortage. Study this chapter thoroughly and you'll never again have to worry about coming home from the slopes, snowball fight, or ice-fishing hole without a Soft Pretzel Braids with Gooey Gouda or Sriracha-Lime Popcorn plan in place. And since suitable attire is of course a close second, priorities-wise, we've also included a handy guide to fireside pastimes, to fill the downtime when roasting chestnuts in a closed oven.

Foolproof Fondue

SERVES 2

Cheesemonger Invitational winner and coauthor of *Cheese Beer Wine Cider: A Field Guide to 75 Perfect Pairings* Steve Jones is a world-renowned cheese savant, so it's no wonder he cracked the code on making a perfect fondue without special equipment. His ingenious technique involves swapping the traditional fondue pot for a small cazuela (a shallow terra-cotta baking dish) and melting the cheese in the oven rather than on the stovetop. If you don't have a cazuela, any oven-safe dish would suit. *Note:* This is a moderate portion, just right for pairing with soup or serving as an appetizer. If you're serving this as a main, or anticipating holiday appetites and wondering if you should double it, just (fon)do it. No one ever complained about too much cheese.

1 garlic clove, halved (optional)
2 tablespoons dry white wine
1 teaspoon cornstarch
1 ounce (28 g) Gruyère cheese, grated
2 ounces (57 g) raclette cheese, grated
Whole nutmeg
4 slices country bread, cut into batons or cubes

AT THE CABIN
- **Cazuela or other small-scale oven-safe dish, such as a mini pie dish or cocotte**

1. Position a rack in the center of the oven and preheat the oven to 400°F (200°C). Rub the inside of a 5½-inch (14 cm) cazuela with the cut side of the garlic clove, if desired, and set it on a rimmed sheet pan. Discard the garlic.

2. Using a fork, mix together the wine and cornstarch in a small bowl to create a slurry. Combine the slurry and cheeses in a separate small bowl and gently stir to coat. Spoon the mixture into the cazuela, and grate nutmeg over the top.

3. Bake for 10 minutes, or until melted and smooth, stirring once around the 7-minute mark and then again when you remove the dish from the oven. Serve immediately, with the bread for dipping.

Alpine Cheese Board

Strike up your cheesemonger's favorite conversation by asking after Alpine cheeses, the large-format (upward of 20 pounds/9 kg) semi-firm unpasteurized cow's-milk cheeses that hail from the mountain range stretching across Europe. These behemoth wheels take on regionally distinct flavors (think: hay, grass, and wildflowers) through transhumance, the practice of grazing cows in the warmer lowlands in the winter and nudging them to cooler highlands come summer. Sample fervently and select your favorites from the case (or ours, below), or let your inner cheese nerd free and explore the influence of microclimates by tasting across a style. Fill your board with crackers and little bowls of cornichons, fig jam, and Dijon mustard, and serve with the wines of the region, malty beers, or crisp cider.

1. Gruyère d'Alpage is made in early autumn when the herd, having spent their summer grazing, returns from the mountain pasture; these centerpiece cheeses are made by small Swiss producers in only a smattering of chalets.

2. Swiss **Chällerhocker**, which literally translates to "sitting in the cellar," is aged at least ten months and is a pleasure of a snacker, creamy and dense, like a dreamy onion tart.

3. A toothsome French **Tomme de Savoie**, which arrives in a small round, is just the cheese to pull from your backpack and slice with a pocketknife during a snowshoe picnic.

4. Scharfe Maxx, a sharp, creamy, Appenzeller-style cheese, was invented after the Swiss

Cheese Union collapsed, allowing a third-generation cheesemaker from Thurgau to break free from the constraints of traditional standards and innovate.

5. We're in it for the looks with **Alp Blossom**, a grassy Austrian cheese covered with summertime flora that will instantly upgrade your cheese board with its showstopping beauty.

6. The year after France's famed raw-milk cheese **Reblochon** was banned from import to the United States, luscious, bloomy-rinded, and, most important, *pasteurized* **Le Délice du Jura** stepped in to take its place on the cheese board, or in a stateside tartiflette.

Fireside Picnic Duck Rillettes

MAKES 2 CUPS (480 ML)

Take your fireside picnic to the next level by adding this wondrous potted spread of slowly poached duck to the charcuterie board. Look for duck legs at specialty butchers, where you can also find duck fat. If you don't wish to buy a tub, you could substitute olive oil; however, once you have duck fat on hand, there's really no end to the exceptional breakfast potatoes you can fry up.

2 Moulard duck legs
(1½ to 2 pounds/
680 to 910 g)
Kosher salt
1 teaspoon whole black
peppercorns
3 garlic cloves,
smashed and peeled
1 bay leaf
3 thyme sprigs
1 cup (240 ml) dry
white wine
1 tablespoon brandy
1 teaspoon grated
orange zest
Freshly ground black
pepper
½ cup (120 ml) duck
fat, melted
Baguette, for serving
Dijon mustard, for
serving (optional)
Cornichons, for serving

AT THE CABIN
- Dutch oven
- Two widemouthed
8-ounce (240 ml)
jars

1. Rub the duck legs all over with 1 tablespoon of salt, wrap in plastic wrap, and refrigerate overnight.

2. The next day, position a rack in the center of the oven and preheat the oven to 250°F (120°C).

3. Nestle the duck legs snugly in a small (4-quart/4 L) enameled Dutch oven and add the peppercorns, garlic, bay leaf, thyme, and wine. Add water to cover. Bake for 3 hours, or until the meat is very tender.

4. Transfer the duck legs to a plate, reserving the liquid in the pot. Shred the meat into a medium bowl, discarding the bones, skin, gristle, and any herbs.

5. Strain the reserved cooking liquid through a fine-mesh sieve set over a spouted bowl. Skim the fat into a liquid measuring cup and set aside. Stir ¼ cup (60 ml) of the liquid, the brandy, and the orange zest into the shredded meat to moisten it. Season with salt and pepper, then pack tightly into two widemouthed 8-ounce (240 ml) jars or small terrines.

6. Measure the reserved duck fat and add additional melted duck fat to make ½ cup (120 ml) total. Pour the fat over the duck rillettes to cover the surface entirely and replace the lids of the jars or terrines. Refrigerate for at least 2 days before serving (the rillettes will keep in the fridge for up to 2 months).

7. To serve, push aside the fat with a butter knife. (It's just there to seal the deal.) Spread on baguette slices (with Dijon mustard, if you like) and top with a cornichon.

Chestnuts Roasting in a Closed Oven

SERVES 4

Few cold-weather delicacies are as evocative as Nat King Cole's "chestnuts roasting on an open fire," but if you're lacking both an open fire and a Parisian street vendor's chestnut-roasting apparatus, worry not. Although this recipe uses a far less romantic oven, the technique makes the business of peeling the chestnuts so much easier, and you can still serve them in a newspaper cone while shouting "Chauds, les marrons chauds!" for dramatic effect. For a decadent fireside snack spread, serve these with a wedge of creamy Cambozola and slices of garlicky pork sausage and fresh ripe pear.

1 pound (455 g) fresh chestnuts
¼ cup (10 g) 1-inch-long (2.5 cm) rosemary sprigs
Zest of 1 small orange, removed with a vegetable peeler in 1-inch-wide (2.5 cm) strips
Flaky sea salt

1. Preheat the oven to 400°F (200°C).

2. Working with one chestnut at a time, very carefully cut an "x" across the chestnut's rounded belly with a sharp paring knife, being sure to slice all the way through the shell. (Do not skip this step, or this recipe will rapidly devolve into "Chestnuts Exploding in a Closed Oven.")

3. Soak the chestnuts in a bowl of hot water for 1 minute. Drain and dry with a kitchen towel. Unfurl a length of aluminum foil and arrange the chestnuts on it in a single layer. Bring the short ends together, leaving enough room for an air pocket, and fold over twice, then fold (don't crumple) in the loose ends to seal the deal. Poke the packet with the paring knife in a few places to allow steam to escape.

4. Roast the chestnuts until the shells peel back and the nut meat is soft and tender (poke it with a fork to check), 15 to 20 minutes. Remove the chestnuts from the oven and wrap them in the slightly damp kitchen towel. Let the nuts sit for a few minutes until they're cool enough to handle, then peel off the shells and papery skin.

5. Crush the rosemary sprigs and orange zest slightly to release the oils, toss them with the warm nuts and a generous pinch of flaky salt, and serve. Save any leftovers (ha) for a decadent chestnut stuffing or soup.

A Jumble of Jars:
Selecting Store-Bought Snacks

Cabin time is an invitation to indulge, so anticipate plowing through the provisions with impressive speed. If you buy in bulk, which we recommend, transfer the goods to quart-size (1 L) mason jars, label them with their contents, and refill nightly, or hourly, depending. Set out with a stack of small bowls, so friends can make their own never-ending sensational snack mixes.

Moose Chow

MAKES ABOUT 5 QUARTS (5 L)

Keep the snack tins well stocked with our take on the make-ahead Midwestern marvel you might know as puppy chow, or muddy buddies, or childhood-by-the-handful. With pecan "hooves," pretzel "snowshoes," coconut "snowflakes," and a blizzard of powdered sugar, it's the most appealing type of wintry mix.

1 (12-ounce/340 g) box Rice Chex cereal

10 ounces (285 g) dark chocolate (70 to 85% cacao), finely chopped

¾ cup (180 ml) almond butter

2 tablespoons coconut oil

½ teaspoon ground cinnamon

1 teaspoon kosher salt

1 teaspoon pure vanilla extract

2 cups (250 g) confectioners' sugar

1 cup (85 g) unsweetened flaked coconut

1½ cups (150 g) raw pecans, toasted

4 cups (480 g) checkerboard-shaped pretzels

1. Pour the Chex into a roasting pan or a giant bowl. Fill a medium saucepan with 2 inches (5 cm) of water and bring to a simmer. Fit a heatproof medium bowl snugly on top, making sure the bottom of the bowl does not touch the water, and place the chocolate, almond butter, coconut oil, cinnamon, and salt in the bowl. Heat, stirring continuously, until melted, well combined, and smooth. Remove from the heat and stir in the vanilla. Pour over the Chex and gently mix with a nonstick spatula until coated. Sift 1 cup (125 g) of the confectioners' sugar on top and toss to coat.

2. Line two rimmed sheet pans with parchment paper and divide the coated Chex between them, spreading the cereal into an even layer. Sift the remaining 1 cup (125 g) confectioners' sugar on top, tossing to coat, until you're nearing the end of the sugar supply; finish with a final snowfall of sugar. Refrigerate for 1 hour or let stand on the counter overnight to set. Use a slotted spoon to return the Chex to the (clean) roasting pan or bowl, shaking off excess sugar. Add the flaked coconut, pecans, and pretzels and toss to combine. Store in an airtight container at room temperature for up to 1 week.

TINY TIP: *If you or your fellow snackers have dietary restrictions, this mix is easy to adapt. Most dark chocolate bars with a high cacao percentage are vegan, but if that's a concern, check the ingredients list to be certain. Make the mix gluten-free by selecting spelt pretzels, or nut-free by swapping in sunflower seed butter and omitting the pecans.*

Whiskey and Bitters Bar Mix

MAKES 3 CUPS (720 ML)

Have your cocktail and eat it, too. This nut mix requires two key ingredients of a classic Manhattan (page 169), our favorite wintertime go-to tipple, so stocking the cabin bar with these supplies (plus vermouth and a jar of cherries!) will keep you well prepared for a season of fireside fortifications.

1 pound (455 g) unsalted raw nuts (a mix of pecans, almonds, walnuts, hazelnuts—whatever you like!)

½ cup (120 ml) bourbon or rye whiskey

¼ cup packed (55 g) brown sugar

1 tablespoon coconut oil

1 tablespoon Worcestershire sauce

½ teaspoon Angostura bitters

1 teaspoon kosher salt

1. Position a rack in the center of the oven and preheat the oven to 325°F (160°C). Line a rimmed sheet pan with parchment paper (for easier cleanup).

2. Combine the mixed nuts in a large bowl.

3. Whisk together the bourbon or whiskey, brown sugar, coconut oil, Worcestershire, bitters, and salt in a medium saucepan. Bring to a boil over medium heat, then reduce the heat to maintain a simmer and cook for 2 minutes, until the initial foaming settles into a glossy syrup. Pour the mixture over the nuts and stir with a nonstick spatula until completely coated.

4. Spread the nuts on the prepared sheet pan and bake for 15 to 20 minutes, stirring midway through the baking time, until the nuts are dry and one shade darker. Remove from the oven and let cool for at least 10 minutes before serving. Store leftover nuts in an airtight container at room temperature for up to 2 weeks.

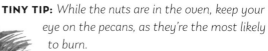

TINY TIP: *While the nuts are in the oven, keep your eye on the pecans, as they're the most likely to burn.*

Five-Spice Candied Cashews

MAKES 2 CUPS (480 ML)

For that friend who has everything, except for a snack to pair with their Yuzu Sour (page 181), might we suggest this dead-simple DIY gift? It's an update of the brown sugar–kissed cashews of Christmases past. This time, the bar nuts are tossed with a dusting of Chinese five-spice powder, which is one of our favorite flavor-bomb cheats when we're on the road and trying to buy fewer ingredients. Hit your grocer's bulk bins to buy just a teaspoon of the spice mix, which traditionally includes star anise, cloves, cinnamon, fennel, and Sichuan pepper. For a variation, rifle through the cupboard to see if there's any pumpkin pie spice or gingerbread spice kicking around.

¼ cup packed (55 g) dark brown sugar
1 teaspoon Chinese five-spice powder
½ teaspoon pure vanilla extract
¼ teaspoon cayenne pepper
1 large egg white, at room temperature
1 teaspoon kosher salt
2 cups (240 g) raw unsalted cashews

1. Position a rack in the center of the oven and preheat the oven to 325°F (160°C). Line a sheet pan with parchment paper (for easier cleanup).

2. Whisk together the brown sugar, five-spice powder, vanilla, and cayenne in a medium bowl.

3. In another medium bowl, whisk together the egg white, salt, and 1 tablespoon water until frothy.

4. Fold the cashews into the egg whites and toss to coat. Transfer to a colander set in the sink to drain for 5 minutes, until shiny but not goopy. Toss the cashews in the sugar-spice mix to coat, then transfer them to the prepared sheet pan.

5. Bake for 30 minutes, stirring once, until toasty brown. Loosen with a spatula and let cool before serving or storing. Store in an airtight container at room temperature for up to 1 week.

Sriracha-Lime Popcorn

MAKES ABOUT 10 CUPS (2.4 L)

When there's sleet running down the cabin window and you have your feet up by the fire, it seems like the best possible time to sip a cold Singha, eat an entire batch of this spicy lime zest–laced popcorn, and plan your summer trip to . . . somewhere warmer. If you can't pop the popcorn fresh due to a stockpot shortage, swap in 10 cups (2.4 L) popped microwave popcorn (about one full-size bag).

1 tablespoon unsalted butter
1 heaping tablespoon sriracha
2 tablespoons coconut oil
⅓ cup (90 g) unpopped popcorn kernels
Zest of 1 large lime
¾ teaspoon kosher salt

1. Melt the butter in a small saucepan over medium-low heat. Stir in the sriracha and set aside.

2. Melt the coconut oil in a large stockpot with a tight-fitting lid over high heat. Add the popcorn kernels and cover the pot. When you hear the first kernel pop, pull the pot from the heat, give it a good swirl, and return it to the burner. Repeat every 10 seconds or so until the popping slows to one pop every few seconds, then remove the pot from the heat.

3. Transfer the popcorn to a large bowl. Slowly drizzle the sriracha-butter mixture over the popcorn, stirring until it's evenly distributed. Sprinkle with the lime zest and salt and toss to combine. Serve immediately.

TINY TIP: *If you're feeling nutty, mix in ½ cup (about 65 g) each of roasted salted cashews and peanuts before serving.*

Go to (Ski) Town Cauliflower Nachos

SERVES 6 TO 8

Roasted cauliflower offers plentiful nooks and crannies for spicy Buffalo dip distribution in these Super Bowl–ready sheet-pan nachos, but if you prefer shredded chicken, aim for 2 cups (280 g).

1 head cauliflower (about 2 pounds/ 1 kg), cut into 1-inch (2.5 cm) florets
2 tablespoons extra-virgin olive oil
Kosher salt and freshly ground black pepper
4 tablespoons (½ stick/ 60 g) unsalted butter
½ cup (120 ml) classic hot sauce, such as Frank's RedHot
1 (14-ounce/400 g) bag restaurant-style corn tortilla chips
12 ounces (340 g) Monterey Jack cheese, freshly grated
½ cup (120 ml) sour cream
2 celery stalks, thinly sliced on an angle
4 radishes, thinly sliced
3 ounces (85 g) blue cheese, crumbled
½ cup (20 g) chopped fresh cilantro leaves

1. Position a rack in the center of the oven and preheat the oven to 450°F (230°C).

2. On a rimmed sheet pan, toss the cauliflower florets with the olive oil to coat. Season with salt and pepper. Bake for 20 minutes, or until the cauliflower is tender with browned, crispy edges.

3. Melt the butter and hot sauce in a large saucepan over low heat, stirring to combine. Remove from the heat. Add the cauliflower to the butter mixture and stir gently to coat.

4. Spread half the bag of chips in a single layer on a sheet pan. Sprinkle with half the Monterey Jack, leaving no chip un-cheesed. Using a slotted spoon, distribute half the cauliflower over the chips. Add the rest of the chips, Monterey Jack, and cauliflower to make a second layer of each.

5. Bake until the cheese has melted, about 5 minutes. Remove from the oven and top with dollops of sour cream. Sprinkle with the celery, radishes, blue cheese, and cilantro. Serve directly from the sheet pan.

Sambal-Spiced Wings with Yuzu Yogurt Dip

SERVES 4 TO 6

Before we tried this dry-brining trick, we considered ourselves rather fry-or-die on chicken wings. Delightfully, these oven-baked wings are actually crispy, making it possible to avoid the hassle of finding the cabin's fire extinguisher just in case frying doesn't go *exactly* as planned, while also ensuring that you (and the only sweater you packed) won't smell like eau de oil forever after. The ticket is a sprinkle of baking powder—just make sure it's aluminum-free to avoid off flavors. (Common aluminum-free baking powder brands include Rumford, Bob's Red Mill, and Trader Joe's.)

YUZU YOGURT DIP

- 1 cup (240 ml) plain full-fat Greek-style yogurt
- 1 tablespoon yuzu juice (substitute fresh lemon juice, if you can't find yuzu)
- 1 tablespoon fresh lime juice
- ½ teaspoon kosher salt

WINGS

- 3 pounds (1.4 kg) chicken wings, tips removed
- 1 tablespoon kosher salt
- 2 teaspoons aluminum-free baking powder
- 2 teaspoons granulated garlic
- ⅓ cup (80 ml) sambal oelek
- ⅓ cup (80 ml) sriracha
- 2 tablespoons honey
- 1 tablespoon fish sauce (optional)
- Sesame seeds, for garnish
- 4 Persian cucumbers or 1 English cucumber, cut into spears
- 4 celery stalks, cut into sticks

1. To make the dip: In a small bowl, stir together the yogurt, yuzu juice, lime juice, and salt. Cover and refrigerate while you make the wings.

2. To make the wings: Line a rimmed sheet pan with aluminum foil.

3. Pat the wings dry with a paper towel and transfer to a large bowl. Combine the salt, baking powder, and granulated garlic in a small bowl, then sprinkle the mixture over the wings and toss to coat. Spread the wings in a single layer on the prepared sheet pan. If making immediately, let stand at room temperature for 1 hour before cooking. (At this point, the wings can also be refrigerated, uncovered, for up to 1 day; let stand at room temperature for 1 hour before baking.)

4. Position one oven rack 4 inches (10 cm) from the broiler and another in the bottom third of the oven. Preheat the oven to 250°F (120°C).

5. Bake the wings on the lower rack for 30 minutes, rotating the pan and flipping the chicken halfway through the cooking time. Move the sheet pan to the top rack and raise the oven temperature to 425°F (220°C). Bake for 30 minutes more, again rotating the pan and flipping the chicken halfway through the cooking time. Remove from the oven and heat the broiler.

6. Whisk together the sambal oelek, sriracha, honey, and fish sauce in a large bowl. Add the cooked wings and toss to coat. Set a wire rack over the sheet pan and use a slotted spoon to set the wings on the rack. Broil the wings for 5 minutes, until the sauce seizes. Remove from the oven.

7. Sprinkle the wings with sesame seeds and transfer to a platter. Serve with the cucumbers, celery, and yuzu yogurt dip.

TINY TIP: *Turn to page 181 for another use for your yuzu juice: hot sake toddies.*

Red Pepper–Walnut Spread and Last of the Cupboard Crackers

MAKES 2 CUPS (480 ML) DIP AND 2 (8-BY-13-INCH/20 BY 33 CM) CRACKERS

This smoky roasted red pepper and walnut spread, a take on Middle Eastern muhammara, is particularly stunning when paired with seeded crackers. We recommend sesame seeds here, since it's generally what we have kicking around, but feel free to make the most of any lingering bits and bobs you have in your kitchen, swapping in a mixture of quinoa, pepitas, sunflower seeds, or any other small seeds lingering in once-full bulk bin bags. If you're not in a cracker-making mood, the dip is also delicious with pita chips or crostini.

SPREAD

3 large red bell peppers
1 cup (4 ounces/115 g) shelled raw walnuts
1 slice sandwich bread, cubed
3 tablespoons extra-virgin olive oil, plus more for drizzling
1 to 2 tablespoons harissa
1 tablespoon pomegranate molasses (see Tiny Tip), plus more for drizzling
1 teaspoon fresh lemon juice
1 teaspoon paprika
1 teaspoon kosher salt
Flaky sea salt, for garnish

1. To make the spread: Position an oven rack in the second highest position and preheat the broiler.

2. Place the bell peppers on a sheet pan and slide them under the broiler (they should be near the broiler heat element but not touching it). Broil the peppers, turning them with tongs every 2 to 3 minutes, until the skin is blackened on all sides. Transfer the peppers to a bowl, cover with a plate, and let cool for at least 15 minutes. Turn the oven to 325°F (160°C) and position a rack in the center.

3. Spread the walnuts on a sheet pan and toast in the oven until fragrant and one shade darker, 10 to 12 minutes. Set aside to cool. (If you're also making crackers, work ahead on step 6 while the nuts are toasting.)

4. Finely chop two walnuts and set aside for garnish. Peel, seed, and coarsely chop the cooled peppers. Pulse the bread cubes in a food processor until broken down into fine crumbs, then add the whole walnuts, the roasted peppers, olive oil, 1 tablespoon harissa, pomegranate molasses, lemon juice, paprika, and kosher salt and purée until smooth. Taste and add more harissa if you'd like it spicier. (If not serving immediately, transfer the spread to an airtight container and store in the refrigerator for up to 5 days.)

SEED CRACKERS

¾ cup (100 g) ground flaxseed

½ cup (75 g) sesame seeds

1 tablespoon tapioca flour or arrowroot powder

1 tablespoon za'atar, or ½ teaspoon kosher salt

¾ cup (180 ml) boiling water

AT THE CABIN

• **Food processor**

5. Transfer the spread to a small wide bowl, make a well in the center, and drizzle a little olive oil and pomegranate molasses over the top. Finish with a sprinkle of the chopped walnuts and some flaky salt.

6. To make the crackers: Stir together the flaxseed, sesame seeds, tapioca flour, and za'atar in a medium bowl. Stir in the boiling water and let stand for 5 minutes.

7. Transfer half the seed mixture to a sheet-pan length of parchment paper set on the countertop. Place another sheet of parchment on top and use a rolling pin to roll the seed mixture into a rough oval, ⅛ inch (3 mm) thick. Transfer to a sheet pan and peel off the top layer of parchment. Repeat with the remaining seed mixture, reusing the top layer of parchment and using a second sheet pan.

8. Bake for 45 minutes, rotating the pans once, until the crackers are dry to the touch and the edges begin to lift from the pan. Remove from the oven and let cool. Use your hands to break the crackers into smaller pieces. Serve with the spread. Store leftover crackers in an airtight container at room temperature for up to 1 month.

TINY TIP: *If you can't find pomegranate molasses, buy pomegranate juice. Bring 1 cup to a low boil in a small saucepan, then cook until it has reduced by half.*

Ollie Ollie Onion Dip

MAKES ABOUT 1½ CUPS (360 ML)

What deviled eggs are to picnics, onion dip is to cabins—that is, practically required. This updated take calls for preserved lemons, one of our favorite pantry staples because they last for ages and pack big flavor. Find them online or in well-stocked grocery stores, or try your hand at making your own. Look to our recipes for braised greens (see page 80) and buttermilk chicken (see page 122) to revisit this ingredient.

1 cup (240 ml) plain full-fat Greek-style yogurt
2 tablespoons finely chopped preserved lemon rind (from 1 preserved lemon, rinsed with water)
½ teaspoon freshly ground black pepper, plus more as needed
2 tablespoons extra-virgin olive oil
2 large red onions, halved and cut lengthwise into ⅛-inch-thick (3 mm) slices (think petals, not rings)
Kosher salt
1 tablespoon brown sugar
Pinch of cayenne pepper
2 tablespoons red wine vinegar
1 teaspoon fresh thyme leaves, plus more for garnish
Flaky sea salt
Pita chips, Fennel Flatbreads (page 81), or crostini (see Tiny Tip), for serving

1. To make the dip: Whisk together the yogurt, preserved lemon, and black pepper in a medium bowl. Cover and refrigerate.

2. Warm the olive oil in a large saucepan over medium-low heat. Add the onions in three batches, stirring now and again and waiting 2 minutes between each addition to allow the onions to soften and make room for more. Season with a pinch of kosher salt and cook for 20 minutes, or until the onions are deep purple and beginning to blacken on the edges. Stir in the brown sugar and cayenne. Add the vinegar and stir, scraping the bottom of the pan to capture any browned bits, then cook for 5 minutes more, until the onions are jammy. Set aside to cool.

3. Transfer the cooled onions to the bowl with the yogurt and stir to combine. Transfer to a serving bowl; sprinkle with thyme, flaky salt, and black pepper; and serve at room temperature with pita chips, Fennel Flatbreads, or crostini.

TINY TIP: *To make crostini, cut a baguette into ¼-inch-thick (6 mm) slices and divide them between two sheet pans. Brush with olive oil, sprinkle with kosher salt, and bake in a preheated 350°F (180°C) oven for 20 to 25 minutes, rotating the pans and flipping the crostini once, until golden brown and crisp.*

MENU

NUT MIX AND CHILL

Take the date-night mood from snowy to snuggly with this swanky steak supper.

Whiskey and Bitters Bar Mix   42

Smoky Cheddar-Pecan Coins   52

Bunny Hill Blue Cheese Wedge   77

Fennel-Gorgonzola Gratin   82

Ski House Steak with Herb Butter   128

Maple Walnut–Whisky Butter Tarts   150

Pinot noir aplenty

Smokey the Pear cocktails   188

Smoky Cheddar-Pecan Coins

MAKES 32

These delicate, buttery cheese crackers come together in minutes, get along very well with wine, and are happiest piled on a cheese board, although you can also just serve them solo with a little jar of apple butter. The cayenne packs a peppery punch; cut back the quantity or omit if you're sensitive to spice. The dough freezes flawlessly, so keep a spare log on standby in the freezer for impromptu parties (whether of one or more). These only get better with age, so if you're prepping for a party, go ahead and make them a day or two ahead of time.

⅓ cup (35 g) pecans
1 cup (125 g)
   all-purpose flour
3 ounces (85 g) sharp
   cheddar cheese,
   grated (about
   1 packed cup)
1 teaspoon smoked
   paprika
¾ teaspoon kosher salt
¼ teaspoon cayenne
   pepper (optional)
⅛ teaspoon freshly
   ground black pepper
½ cup (1 stick/115 g)
   cold unsalted butter,
   cut into cubes

1. Heat the pecans in a small dry skillet over medium-low heat, tossing often (don't let them burn!), until toasted, about 5 minutes. Remove from the heat and let the pecans cool completely, then transfer to a food processor and pulse to grind them into a coarse meal, 10 to 15 seconds. Add the flour, cheese, paprika, salt, cayenne, and black pepper and process into coarse crumbs. Add the butter and process until the mixture forms a moist, sandy dough that sticks together when you pinch it.

2. Transfer the dough to a piece of plastic wrap. Gather the crumbs together, pressing them firmly into a log. Use the plastic wrap to help shape and roll the log until it's roughly 1½ by 8 inches (4 by 20 cm). Chill the dough for at least 30 minutes and up to 3 days. (The dough can also be frozen for up to 1 month; let it sit out at room temperature until pliable before slicing, to prevent cracking when you cut it.)

3. When ready to bake the crackers, preheat the oven to 350°F (180°C). Line a rimmed half sheet pan with parchment paper.

4. Slice the dough into ¼-inch-thick (6 mm) rounds and arrange them on the prepared sheet pan about 1 inch (2.5 cm) apart. Bake the crackers until light and crisp, about 18 minutes. Remove from the oven and let cool completely on the pan. Store the crackers in an airtight container at room temperature for up to 3 days or in the freezer for up to 1 month.

One Fine Tinned Fish-nic

If you haven't already, it's time to embrace the humble tinned fish, that oh-so-fetchingly packaged, effortlessly chic European snack staple. When prepping for a post-alp-summiting happy hour, in lieu of charcuterie and cheese, assemble a simple, splendid spread of silvery sardines and savory smoked shellfish, paired with a fintastic assortment of accoutrements.

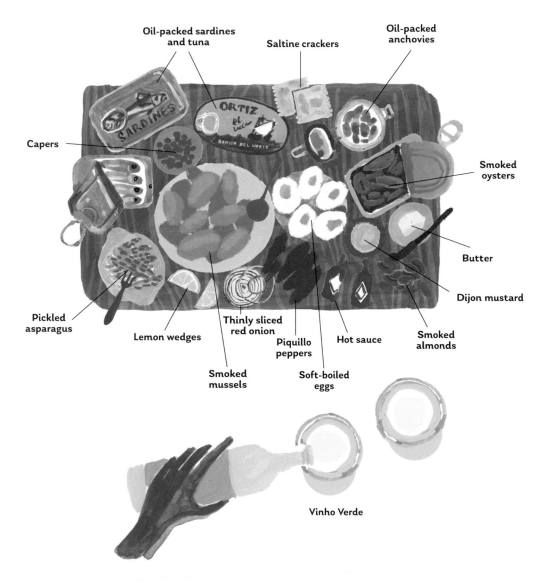

Oil-packed sardines and tuna

Saltine crackers

Oil-packed anchovies

Capers

Smoked oysters

Butter

Dijon mustard

Pickled asparagus

Lemon wedges

Thinly sliced red onion

Piquillo peppers

Hot sauce

Smoked almonds

Smoked mussels

Soft-boiled eggs

Vinho Verde

Soft Pretzel Braids with Gooey Gouda

MAKES 8

Shape this versatile dough however your heart desires, but know that our extensive research indicates that when it comes to dipping, the more tear-off-able crooks, the better, and therefore, a braid will always beat the traditional twist. For sandwich-size pretzel braids, divide the dough into 6 (rather than 8) pieces before shaping.

PRETZEL BRAIDS

1 cup (240 ml) warm water (110° to 115°F/43° to 46°C)
1 tablespoon dark brown sugar
1 package active dry yeast (about 2¼ teaspoons)
3 cups (405 g) unbleached bread flour, plus more for dusting
2 tablespoons unsalted butter, melted and cooled
2 teaspoons kosher salt
Neutral oil, such as grapeseed or sunflower, for greasing
½ cup (90 g) baking soda
1 large egg yolk, beaten with 1 tablespoon water, for egg wash
Coarse salt, for sprinkling
Maple Whole-Grain Mustard (see page 56) or Gooey Gouda (recipe follows), for serving

1. Combine the warm water and brown sugar in the bowl of a stand mixer and sprinkle the yeast on top. Let stand for 8 minutes, until foamy. Add the flour, melted butter, and salt. Using the dough hook attachment, stir until combined, then increase the speed to medium-low and knead for 5 minutes, until the dough is smooth and pulls away from the sides of the bowl.

2. Grease a large bowl with oil and transfer the dough to the bowl. Cover with a kitchen towel and place in the warmest spot in the kitchen to rise for 2 hours, until the dough has doubled in size. (Alternatively, cover the bowl with reusable wrap and refrigerate the dough for up to 2 days before forming and baking the pretzels.)

3. Line two sheet pans with parchment paper. Turn the dough out onto a lightly floured counter. Cut the dough into 8 pieces with a knife or pastry scraper. One at a time, using your hands, roll a piece of dough into a 2-foot-long (60 cm) rope, starting at the center and moving your fingertips outward. Cut the rope into thirds, arrange the pieces side by side, and press the ends together at the top. Braid the strands, tucking under the bottom ends and giving them a little pinch so they don't pop back out. Place the braid on a prepared sheet pan and repeat with the remaining pieces of dough. Let the braids rise for 30 minutes.

4. Position a rack in the center of the oven and preheat the oven to 450°F (230°C).

5. Combine 8 cups (2 L) water and the baking soda in a wide Dutch oven and bring to a boil. Using a skimmer or metal spatula, gently slide the pretzels into the baking soda bath and boil for 30 seconds. Flip and boil for an additional 30 seconds, then return the pretzels to the sheet pan, letting any excess water run off each as you remove it from the pot.

6. Brush each pretzel with the egg wash, then sprinkle with coarse salt. Bake until deeply browned, 10 to 12 minutes, rotating the pans halfway through. Serve with mustard or Gooey Gouda for dipping.

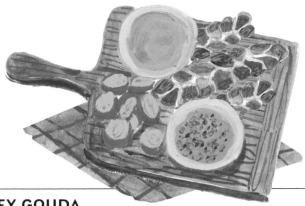

GOOEY GOUDA
MAKES 2½ CUPS (600 ML)

1 cup (240 ml) lager-style beer, such as Old German
¾ cup (180 ml) heavy cream
¾ cup (180 ml) whole milk
1 small white onion, coarsely chopped
2 teaspoons cornstarch
6 ounces (170 g) young Gouda cheese (red wax removed), grated
4 ounces (115 g) American cheese, cut into pieces
½ teaspoon kosher salt
⅛ teaspoon freshly ground white pepper
Freshly grated nutmeg

1. Combine the beer, cream, milk, and onion in a large saucepan. Bring to a boil over medium-high heat, then reduce the heat to maintain a simmer and cook for 10 minutes. Strain through a fine-mesh sieve set over a spouted measuring cup and discard the solids.

2. Return all but ¼ cup (60 ml) of the hot cream mixture to the saucepan. To the reserved cream, add the cornstarch and mix with a fork to make a slurry. Pour the slurry into the saucepan, bring to a boil over medium-high heat, then reduce the heat to low and simmer for 3 minutes to thicken.

3. Stir in the Gouda and American cheese gradually, letting each addition melt before adding the next. Stir in the salt and white pepper. Transfer to a bowl, grate nutmeg on top, and serve, or let cool and store in an airtight container in the refrigerator for up to 3 days (rewarm over low heat before serving).

Kick-Sled Kielbasa with Maple Whole-Grain Mustard

SERVES 4

When Soft Pretzel Braids with Gooey Gouda (page 54) are coming to the party, fill out the guest list with the friends they love to see on the platter—sliced apples, pickled vegetables, and this five-minute sausage-and-mustard duo.

MAPLE WHOLE-GRAIN MUSTARD

½ cup (120 ml) whole-grain mustard
¼ cup (60 ml) pilsner
2 tablespoons Dijon mustard
1 tablespoon pure maple syrup

1 kielbasa with a natural casing, such as Olympia Provisions

1. To make the maple mustard: Whisk together the whole-grain mustard, beer, Dijon, and maple syrup in a small bowl.

2. Position an oven rack 4 inches (10 cm) from the broiler heat element and preheat the broiler.

3. Set the kielbasa on a rimmed sheet pan and broil for 5 minutes, turning once, until the casing crisps and the sausage is warmed through. Slice the kielbasa crosswise into 1-inch (2.5 cm) segments and pile on a platter. Serve with toothpicks and the bowl of mustard alongside.

TINY TIP: *Prefer form over function? For the prettiest kielbasa (now, there are two words you never thought you'd see together!), hasselback your sausage by placing it between two chopsticks and slicing every ½ inch (1.2 cm) before popping it in the oven.*

Cabin Attire

Packing for a wintertime week away calls for a divided approach to outfitting. On the one mitten-clad hand, you're readying yourself for arctic outdoors action, with all the base layers, outer layers, and accessories required to avoid hypothermia. On the other toddy-holding hand, you're preparing for cozy indoor activities calling for the sartorial equivalent of a snuggle. Heed these packing tips to address both scenarios.

Don't Sweat(er) the Small Stuff

Fitted sweaters are fine for layering under your coat, but when inside, the overriding knitwear principle is that bigger = better. If you can't pull the sleeves over your hands to fashion spontaneous mittens, what are you even doing?

The Elastic Brain

The road to relaxation starts with yoga . . . pants. Forgo all restrictive waistbands and belts in favor of stretchy, forgiving fabrics, whether forging the wilderness in your wondrously wicking base layer or lounging by the fire in your athleisure. (Emphasis on "leisure.")

Plaid-itudes

Trends come and go, but in the cabin, flannel is forever.

Stocking Fillers

Be sure to pack snow boots, thermal socks, shearling slippers, and, with calculated risk for early-days romantic relationships, footed pajamas.

Smoke Detector

To rid your jams (and any other non-woolens) of a fire-smoke smell, add 1 cup (240 ml) white vinegar and 1 cup (180 g) baking soda to the washing machine water and soak for 1 hour before washing with hot water.

Protective Outer Layer

Outside, spilled glogg will magically bead up and drip off your coat thanks to the wonders of waterproofing. Inside, without tech fabric, you're toast. Tuck an apron into your duffel, or designate a hoodie to be sacrificed to the kitchen gods.

Pom-Pom Squad

For the duration of the vacation, the hairbrush is out, the woolly hat is in.

Less Is More (Room for Whiskey)

The ambitious will pack numerous coordinated outfits for the cabin, but the wise will pack pajamas, lots of pajamas, knowing they will be their round-the-clock preference and that the suitcase space would be better allotted to a bottle, a board game, or copies of this book.

Snowbound Stromboli with Arrabbiata Sauce

SERVES 4

Take your childhood Hot Pocket crush to adult levels with a spicy arrabbiata dipping sauce, upgraded cured meats, and briny oil-cured olives. This recipe makes small (handful-size) slices of stromboli, so you can pile around the fire and balance a drink, too. If you're cooking for a spice-sensitive crowd, omit the red pepper flakes.

ARRABBIATA SAUCE

1 recipe Red Sauce (see page 126)
2 garlic cloves, grated on a Microplane
1½ teaspoons red pepper flakes

DOUGH

1 cup (240 ml) warm water (110° to 115°F/43° to 46°C)
Extra-virgin olive oil
1 teaspoon honey
2¼ cups (305 g) bread flour, plus more for dusting
1 teaspoon active dry yeast
1 teaspoon kosher salt

STROMBOLI

6 ounces (170 g) whole-milk mozzarella, grated
4 ounces (115 g) soppressata
2 ounces (57 g) pepperoni
2 ounces (57 g) oil-cured olives, pitted and torn
1 ounce (28 g) Parmesan cheese, finely grated
½ teaspoon garlic powder

1. To make the arrabbiata sauce: Follow the instructions to cook the red sauce, adding the additional garlic and red pepper flakes when garlic is called for in the recipe.

2. To make the dough: Whisk together the warm water, 2 tablespoons olive oil, and the honey in a small bowl.

3. Pulse the flour, yeast, and salt in a food processor until combined, about 5 seconds. Add the wet ingredients and process until a dough ball forms, 15 to 20 seconds, then process the dough for 10 to 15 seconds more.

4. Turn the dough out onto a lightly floured counter. Knead the dough for a few seconds, then divide the dough in half. Working with one piece at a time, tuck the edges under to form a ball and place each ball in a bowl. Cover both bowls with kitchen towels and set

them in the warmest area of the kitchen for 1 hour, or until the dough has doubled in size. (If making ahead, transfer each ball of dough to a quart-size [1 L] container and refrigerate for up to 2 days. Let the dough rest at room temperature for an hour before rolling it out.)

5. To assemble the stromboli: Position racks in the top and bottom thirds of the oven and preheat the oven to 375°F (190°C). Line a sheet pan with parchment paper.

6. Flour the counter. With floured hands, transfer one ball of dough to the counter and use a rolling pin to roll it out into a 6-by-14-inch (15 by 35 cm) rectangle. Spread a generous portion of the arrabbiata sauce in the middle of the rectangle, stopping an inch (2.5 cm) shy of the edges. Mentally (or actually) divide the mozzarella, soppressata, pepperoni, and olives into two piles, one for each portion of dough. Layer the mozzarella, soppressata, olives, more mozzarella, and pepperoni over the sauce. Roll the dough lengthwise into a log, tuck the short ends under, and transfer seam-side down to the sheet pan. Repeat with the remaining dough and fillings. Brush both stromboli with olive oil and sprinkle evenly with the Parmesan and garlic powder.

7. Bake for 20 minutes until nicely browned. Remove from the oven and let rest for 5 minutes, then slice crosswise into 2-inch-thick (5 cm) sections. Serve with a side of arrabbiata sauce in a bowl for dipping.

TINY TIP: *Extra arrabbiata sauce is particularly grand when used as the base of a shakshuka, so double the recipe if you're planning ahead. To make shakshuka, cook half an onion and a small red bell pepper in a skillet, pour in the leftover sauce, and bring to simmer. Make 2 to 4 wells in the sauce with a ladle or the back of a spoon and crack an egg into each well. Top with crumbled feta cheese. Bake in a preheated 350°F (180°C) oven until the egg whites are set, about 10 minutes.*

Teeny Blini with Herby Horseradish Crème Fraîche

MAKES ABOUT 50 (2-INCH/5 CM) BLINI

Whether you're celebrating the winter solstice on Wachusett Mountain or New Year's Eve at Nub's Nob, these buckwheat-flour-fortified blini come together in a snap, leaving more time for champagne sipping. How big you make your blini is subjective; we like them bite-size, but if you prefer a two- or three-bite blini, use a tablespoon of batter for each (you'll end up with about 30 blini) and adjust the garnish accordingly. Four ounces (115 g) of smoked salmon allows for about a postage-stamp-size piece per pancake; if that sounds anticlimactic, double up.

CRÈME FRAÎCHE TOPPING

1 (8-ounce/225 g) container crème fraîche
¼ cup (13 g) finely chopped fresh dill
2 tablespoons finely chopped fresh parsley
2 tablespoons freshly grated horseradish
1 teaspoon grated lemon zest
½ teaspoon kosher salt
¼ teaspoon freshly ground black pepper

BLINI

2 tablespoons unsalted butter, plus more for greasing
½ cup (65 g) all-purpose flour
¼ cup (30 g) buckwheat flour
½ teaspoon baking soda
¼ teaspoon kosher salt
1 cup (240 ml) buttermilk
1 large egg

1. Line a rimmed half sheet pan with a kitchen towel.

2. To make the crème fraîche topping: Mix together the crème fraîche, dill, parsley, horseradish, lemon zest, salt, and pepper in a small bowl, then cover and refrigerate until ready to use (it will keep for up to 2 days).

3. To make the blini: Melt the butter in a large skillet over low heat. Remove from the heat and let cool slightly. Mix together the all-purpose flour, buckwheat flour, baking soda, and salt in a small bowl. Mix together the buttermilk, egg, and melted butter (don't clean the skillet—you're going to reuse it) in a small bowl. Add the wet ingredients to the dry ingredients and mix until just combined.

4. Heat the reserved skillet over medium heat and grease it generously with butter. Pour heaping teaspoonfuls of batter into the skillet (fit in as many as possible without letting them touch). Cook the blini until crisped, golden, and baked through, 2 to 3 minutes per side (the exact timing will depend on how hot your pan is; don't let it get too hot, or the blini will blacken). Transfer the blini to the prepared sheet pan and cover them with the towel. Repeat with the remaining batter, buttering the pan between batches.

TO SERVE

4 to 8 ounces
(115 to 225 g)
cold-smoked salmon
50 paper-thin English
cucumber slices
(about ¼ cucumber)
50 tiny fresh dill
fronds
2 tablespoons minced
fresh chives
Freshly ground black
pepper

5. When ready to serve, arrange the blini in rows on a large platter. Garnish each with 1 teaspoon of the crème fraîche topping, a piece of smoked salmon, a slice of cucumber, a dill frond, a pinch of chives, and a pinch of pepper.

TINY TIPS: *In lieu of serving the blini already garnished, you can set out a GIY (garnish-it-yourself) blini bar, with bowls of crème fraîche or sour cream, grated red and golden beets, chopped hard-boiled egg, halved soft-boiled quail eggs, minced red onion or shallot, minced chives or scallions, fresh herbs (minced, whole leaves, or fronds), capers, lemon zest, microgreens, fish roe, and, if your snow-day posse is particularly posh, fancy caviar.*

No time/motivation to make blini? Use good-quality thick-cut potato chips instead.

Sausage Rolls with Pear-Sultana Chutney

MAKES 26 (1-INCH/2.5 CM) ROLLS

There's really very little that can go wrong any time you're wrapping something delicious (sausage) in something extra delicious (pastry). In American grocery stores, the pork sausage behind the butcher counter is often seasoned. If you can't find unseasoned pork sausage (often packaged in a tube, near the bacon), purchase sweet sausages from the case, squeeze the sausage out of the links, and skip to step 4.

1½ teaspoons fennel seeds
1 tablespoon extra-virgin olive oil
1 small onion, finely chopped
1 garlic clove, minced
12 ounces (340 g) ground pork sausage
2 tablespoons finely chopped sultanas (golden raisins)
1 tablespoon minced fresh sage
¾ teaspoon kosher salt
½ teaspoon freshly ground black pepper
Pinch of freshly grated nutmeg
1 sheet frozen puff pastry (from a 17.3-ounce/490 g package), thawed according to the package directions
1 egg, beaten with 1 tablespoon milk, for egg wash
Sesame seeds, for sprinkling
Pear-Sultana Chutney (recipe follows), for serving

1. Position a rack in the center of the oven and preheat the oven to 350°F (180°C). Line a sheet pan with parchment paper.

2. Swirl the fennel seeds in a dry skillet over medium heat until fragrant. Crush with a mortar and pestle or spice grinder. Warm the olive oil in the skillet over medium-low heat. Add the onion and cook, stirring often, until tender, about 5 minutes. Add the garlic and cook just until fragrant, 1 minute. Remove from the heat and let cool.

3. Transfer the onion mixture to a large bowl and add the sausage, sultanas, sage, salt, pepper, and nutmeg, then use clean hands to mix the ingredients together. Wash your hands.

4. On a lightly floured countertop, roll the puff pastry sheet to a 9-by-24-inch (23 by 61 cm) rectangle about ⅛ inch (3 mm) thick. Cut it in half lengthwise and crosswise, and use your hands to compress the sausage into a cylinder down the middle of each piece of pastry. Brush the edges of the pastry with the egg wash and firmly fold one side over the other. Flip it over, so the seam is down, and slice into 1-inch-wide (2.5 cm) segments. Transfer to the prepared sheet pan, taking care to leave space between the rolls.

5. Brush each roll with the egg wash, sprinkle with sesame seeds, and bake for 25 to 30 minutes until puffed and golden. Serve warm, with the chutney.

PEAR-SULTANA CHUTNEY

MAKES 1½ CUPS (360 ML)

¼ cup (120 ml) apple cider vinegar
¼ cup packed (55 g) brown sugar
3 large pears, peeled, cored, and cut into ½-inch (1.2 cm) dice
4 Medjool dates, pitted and chopped
¼ cup finely chopped sweet onion
¼ cup (35 g) sultanas (golden raisins)
1 cinnamon stick
1 bay leaf
1 star anise pod
1 (1-inch/2.5 cm) piece fresh ginger, sliced lengthwise
½ teaspoon kosher salt

1. Combine ¾ cup (180 ml) water, the vinegar, brown sugar, pears, dates, onion, sultanas, cinnamon stick, bay leaf, star anise, ginger, and salt in a medium saucepan. Bring to a boil over high heat, then reduce the heat to low and cook, partially covered, for 35 to 40 minutes, or until the chutney is thick and glossy. Remove and discard the whole spices and ginger.

2. Transfer to a bowl with a small spoon for serving or let cool completely and store in an airtight container in the refrigerator for up to 1 month. (Use extra chutney as a topping for pork tenderloin or as a spread for a turkey sandwich with cream cheese and arugula.)

TINY TIP: *If you're pressed for time, or do not cherish chutney, Maple Whole-Grain Mustard (see page 56) is also a delicious dip.*

Having a Cheese Ball: A Retro Revival

ALL BALLS SERVE 4 TO 6 LACTOSE LOVERS

Your Rocky Mountain A-frame has dark wood–paneled walls, lustrous orange-and-brown shag carpet, lime-green wicker lampshades, and a startlingly floral sofa—now all you need is the throwback party snack to match. Enter the humble but beloved cheese ball, table topper of honor at swinging cocktail parties of yore, and still one of the most stalwart scene-stealing appetizers around (especially when shaped like a red fox). Here are a few tips on cheese ball composition, creativity, and companionship, plus four fantastic cheese balls guaranteed to get a roll lotta love.

Get the Ball Rolling
The basic cheese ball blueprint consists of cream cheese, grated cheddar, chopped nuts, scallions, spices, and a splash of Worcestershire blended, shaped into a ball, and rolled in more chopped nuts and fresh herbs. It's tough to botch a cheese ball, so have some fun and experiment with Gorgonzola, Gouda, and goat cheese; mix in everything from bacon and black sesame seeds to cumin and curry; and when it comes time to roll, debate the merits of pecans versus pistachios, thyme versus tarragon, dried cranberries versus crushed pretzels, and pineapple-shaped versus pinecone-shaped.

Roll Models
If you're short on time and/or ingredients, make a quick batch of mini balls: start with a soft, smooth log of goat cheese; form individual balls roughly 1½ inches (4 cm) in diameter; and roll them in your chosen garnish—finely chopped nuts, fresh herbs, black and white sesame seeds, grated citrus zest, or black pepper. Or for a particularly fetching floral display, press edible pansies, chive blossoms, kale flowers, or tiny mint and basil leaves into the surface.

Puttin' on the Ritz
Creamy cheese balls and crispy crackers go together like eggnog and rum, flickering fires and faux sheepskin rugs, a snow shovel and anyone but you. And while we've yet to meet a cracker we don't want to dip into or smear with cheese, it's pretty much universally accepted that Ritz are the consummate cheese ball companion. For a too-delicate-to-dip but quite delicious cheese plate pairing, bake up a log of Smoky Cheddar-Pecan Coins (page 52).

Fresh Take
If you're going gluten-free, or just trying to balance out all that decadent cheese, accent your cheese ball platter with fresh, brightly colored crudités: snappy celery and carrot sticks, blanched asparagus and green beans, halved radishes, sliced bell peppers, Persian cucumber spears, and sweet little cherry tomatoes.

Let's Roll

Before you begin, let the cream cheese and goat cheese come to room temperature so they're easier to work with. After blending the recipe components using a spatula or mixer, shape the mixture into a ball and gently roll it in the garnish, or decorate as instructed. Serve immediately, or chill until ready to serve (don't wait too long, lest the garnish get soggy).

If planning ahead, form the ball, double wrap it in plastic wrap sans garnish, and refrigerate it for up to 5 days. Come party time, let the ball sit out for 15 to 30 minutes to soften, then roll it in the garnish or decorate as instructed. Serve it with a small knife for spreading.

PA RUM POM POM POM

Mix together 8 ounces (225 g) cream cheese + 3 ounces (85 g) Gorgonzola + ½ cup (55 g) grated white cheddar + ½ cup (60 g) finely chopped toasted walnuts + 1 tablespoon minced fresh thyme + 1 teaspoon freshly ground black pepper; shape into a ball; roll (gently) in 1 cup (175 g) pomegranate arils.

KIND OF A BIG DILL

Mix together 4 ounces (115 g) cream cheese + 4 ounces (115 g) goat cheese + 4 ounces (115 g) feta + ¼ cup (35 g) finely chopped pitted kalamata olives + ¼ cup (30 g) finely chopped pistachios + 2 tablespoons finely chopped fresh dill + 1 teaspoon grated lemon zest; shape into a ball; roll in a mixture of ¼ cup (13 g) finely chopped fresh dill + ¼ cup (30 g) finely chopped pistachios + 2 teaspoons grated lemon zest.

PIMENTÓN CONE

Mix together 8 ounces (225 g) cream cheese + 1 cup (115 g) grated sharp cheddar + ½ cup (70 g) finely chopped smoked almonds + 1 tablespoon finely chopped fresh rosemary + 1 teaspoon smoked paprika; shape into a teardrop; garnish with 1 cup (140 g) smoked almonds arranged like pinecone scales, and rosemary sprigs.

FOX AND LOX

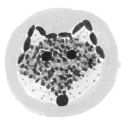

Mix together 8 ounces (225 g) cream cheese + 4 ounces (115 g) goat cheese + 4 ounces (115 g) finely chopped smoked salmon + ¼ cup (11 g) finely chopped scallions + 2 tablespoons finely chopped capers + 1 teaspoon grated lemon zest; shape into a circle with two pointy "ears"; garnish with whole pecans to outline the ears and chopped pecans to fill in the face, a halved black olive for the eyes, and a whole black olive for the nose.

The Never Bored Game

Whether you have a panache for puzzling or a flair for bread-baking or you're a fair- (that is, foul-) weather knitter, there's a fireside activity for you. Roll the dice to start your indoor adventure.

HOME

Coloring Canyon

Empire of Embroidery

Winter Wreath

START

Cookie

Cabin Sweet Cabin

Sourdough Sinkhole

Jigsaw Jungle

Mug Cocktail Mountain

Heath

ZEROPROOF PASS

Knitty City

Quarry

Smashed Potatoes with Caviar and Sour Cream

MAKES ABOUT 16

Dressed up with caviar and sour cream, these fancy party potatoes are a worthy accompaniment to your flute of champagne. Pass them as an appetizer or serve as a first course. If you're not craving caviar, swap in chopped oil-cured olives and Calabrian peppers, parsley and grated lemon zest, or Parmesan and crispy bacon.

1½ pounds (680 g) small Yukon Gold potatoes (16 or so)
Kosher salt
¼ cup (60 ml) extra-virgin olive oil
Freshly ground black pepper
¼ cup (60 ml) sour cream or crème fraîche
1 ounce (28 g) wild salmon roe
1 tablespoon snipped fresh chives

1. Preheat the oven to 425°F (220°C).

2. Put the potatoes in a large pot, fill with water to cover, and generously salt the water. Bring to a boil over high heat, then boil the potatoes until fork-tender and cooked through, 15 to 20 minutes, depending on their size. Drain the potatoes and transfer to a rimmed sheet pan to cool for at least 5 minutes.

3. Use the bottom of a mug to gently but firmly smash each potato to a ½-inch (1.2 cm) thickness. Drizzle with the olive oil and season with salt and pepper. Bake the potatoes for 45 to 60 minutes, flipping them after 20 minutes, until golden and very crispy. (If they're not finished after 45 minutes, flip them every 5 minutes until they are done.)

4. Transfer the potatoes to a serving platter (or plate them individually) and top with dollops of the sour cream and salmon roe. Sprinkle with the chives and serve.

TINY TIP: *If you're the plan-ahead type, the potatoes can be parboiled a day ahead and stored in an airtight container. If you're the scrambling-at-the-last-minute type, you could swap thick potato chips for the smashers and hear exactly zero complaints.*

Lodge Lunch

Never again let lunch be the letdown of your ski day. When you pack your own brown paper sack, you can be absolutely certain of a scrumptious selection that won't leave you feeling like your wallet was mugged on the mountaintop. Store your lunch in a day locker, or keep your itinerary loose by packing it in your backpack. (Ditch the thermos, though—it'll slow you down.) In the time you'll save by not waiting in line for a $50 cup of so-so soup, you can stalk that elusive fireside table and/or hit the bar for a glass of wine or a fortifying hot cocktail, preferably topped with an absurd amount of whipped cream. While there are aspects of the lodge experience we prefer to skirt, there are others we'd never want to do without.

1. Thermos of piping-hot Roasted Kabocha Squash Soup (page 100) **2.** Marcona almonds **3.** Ham sam (butter, Dijon mustard, ham, and Gruyère on a pretzel braid; see page 54) **4.** Crunchy kettle-cooked potato chips **5.** Dark chocolate bar (70% cacao or higher), to propel you into the afternoon **6.** Shiny apple **7.** Wine, if you're calling it a half day

CHAPTER 3

Sides and Salads

A hockey skater needs laces, an ice fisher needs an auger, a winter swimmer needs a thermos of hot buttered bourbon, and a main course needs a side dish (or three). Frosty winter nights call for belly-warming Fennel-Gorgonzola Gratin and platters of piping-hot Coal-Baked Sweet Potatoes with Orange Whiskey Butter, deep baskets of doughy Butter Buns slathered in salted honey butter, and piles of perfectly puffy just-baked popovers. Root vegetables and winter greens get their moment in the sun (er, snow?) with a bright ginger-and-citrus-kissed Carrot-Kohlrabi Slaw, no cast-iron-skillet-seared steak can resist the Bunny Hill Blue Cheese Wedge, and humble chicories may just steal the supper show when tossed into a Radicchio, Persimmon, and Maple Pecan Salad. And since every beautifully balanced dinner needs great conversation, discuss the nuances of tracking both polar bears and polar plungers with the help of our illustrated guide to common animal snow tracks.

Six "Skål!"-Worthy Smørrebrød

Sentiments on salted licorice aside, the Danish have always delivered on deliciousness: akvavit, aebleskiver (see page 196), and that much-loved lunch staple smørrebrød—open-faced sandwiches built on slim slices of rugbrød, a dense brick of dark, chewy, seed-strewn rye bread. Prep a crowd-pleasing lunch by mixing and matching smørrebrød and serving them preassembled on a platter, or lay out ingredients and have everyone engineer their own. Perhaps most important, before eating, raise your shots of akvavit, and "Skål!" like you mean it.

The literal translation of *smørrebrød* is "butter (*smør*) and bread (*brød*)," so begin with a ¼-inch (6 mm) slice of rugbrød (if you can't find it, use a hearty rye or whole-grain bread) and a generous smear of good-quality butter (Lurpak, if it's available), then run with your wildest whims. Here are a handful of starter smørrebrød to set you on the path to open-faced sandwich greatness.

1. Smoked salmon
+ sliced roasted beets + shaved fennel +
capers + chopped fresh dill

2. Avocado
+ bay shrimp + thinly sliced radishes +
chopped fresh chives +
flaky sea salt + lemon wedge

3. Roast beef

+ sliced boiled Yukon Gold potatoes +
sliced dill pickles + grated fresh horseradish

4. Fried cod

+ shaved red cabbage + remoulade +
fresh dill fronds + grated lemon zest

5. Soft-scrambled eggs

+ wild mushrooms sautéed with minced
fresh thyme + chopped fresh parsley

6. Pickled herring

+ sliced hard-boiled egg + sliced cucumber +
shaved red onion + chopped fresh dill

Snowdrift Salad with Anchovy Bread Crumbs

SERVES 4

The heart-quickening beauty of fresh powder visits the supper table when finely grated pecorino falls onto winter greens. Grate this salty sheep's-milk cheese with a Microplane grater for the driftiest effect, and layer in tiny crunchy croutons. If you don't love anchovies, omit them and carry on.

¼ cup plus
   2 tablespoons
   (90 ml) extra-virgin
   olive oil
2 tablespoons fresh
   lemon juice
2 anchovy fillets, or
   1 teaspoon anchovy
   paste
1 garlic clove, minced
1 cup (45 g) fresh
   bread crumbs
   (from crusty bread,
   pulsed in a food
   processor)
1 head frisée
   (see Tiny Tip)
2 ounces (57 g)
   Pecorino Romano
   cheese

AT THE CABIN
- **Microplane grater**

1. Whisk together ¼ cup (60 ml) of the olive oil and the lemon juice in a large salad bowl.

2. Warm the remaining 2 tablespoons olive oil in a medium skillet over medium heat until hot but not smoking. Add the anchovies and stir until they have dissolved. Add the garlic and cook for 30 seconds, until fragrant. Stir in the bread crumbs and cook, tossing often to coat, for 5 minutes, until crisp and toasty brown. Remove from the heat and cool.

3. Just before serving, add the frisée to the bowl with the lemon dressing and, using tongs, toss to coat. Transfer half the frisée to a platter and sprinkle with half the bread crumbs. Grate half the pecorino over the top. Repeat with the remaining frisée, bread crumbs, and cheese and serve.

TINY TIP: *Frisée (also known as curly endive) appears in markets in late winter. Substitute 8 cups (160 g) arugula or chopped romaine hearts if frisée is not available.*

Carrot-Kohlrabi Slaw with Ginger-Sesame Dressing

SERVES 6

If the tedium of julienning by hand makes you feel like a snowbound Jack Nicholson in *The Shining*, use a mandoline or julienne peeler to turn the fruits and vegetables into matchsticks in minutes.

DRESSING

1 teaspoon grated lemon zest
¼ cup (60 ml) fresh lemon juice
2 tablespoons fresh orange juice
2 tablespoons grated fresh ginger
2 tablespoons honey
1 tablespoon toasted sesame oil
¼ cup (60 ml) extra-virgin olive oil
Kosher salt and freshly ground black pepper

SLAW

4 carrots, julienned (about ½ pound)
2 kohlrabi (see Tiny Tip), peeled and grated
1 large parsnip, peeled and julienned
1 large apple, peeled, cored, and julienned
1 small golden beet, peeled and grated
1 bunch kale leaves, stemmed and finely chopped (about 2 cups/130 g)
1 bunch cilantro, coarsely chopped
¾ cup (110 g) golden raisins
½ cup (70 g) coarsely chopped roasted almonds
2 tablespoons minced fresh chives
1 tablespoon black sesame seeds

1. To make the dressing: Whisk together the lemon zest, lemon juice, orange juice, ginger, honey, and sesame oil in a small bowl. While whisking, slowly add the olive oil in a thin stream and whisk until emulsified. Season with salt and pepper.

2. To make the slaw: Toss together the carrots, kohlrabi, parsnip, apple, beet, kale, cilantro, and raisins in a very large bowl. Drizzle the dressing over the vegetables and gently toss to combine. Add salt to taste. Transfer to a serving bowl or platter; garnish with the almonds, chives, and sesame seeds; and serve. If not serving the slaw immediately, transfer it to an airtight container and store in the refrigerator for up to 5 days.

TINY TIP: *If you can't find kohlrabi or are frightened by its otherworldly appearance, try radishes or turnips instead.*

Radicchio, Persimmon, and Maple Pecan Salad

SERVES 4

Bitter, beautiful radicchio warms our cold winter hearts, especially when tempered with a sweet pop of persimmon (use a Fuyu—they're delicious whether firm and crisp or sweet and soft). Experiment with mixing and matching radicchio varieties, from classic reddish-purple Chioggia to frilly pink-speckled Castelfranco; the contrast is gorgeous. If you love chicory's bite—the more bitter, the better—skip the soak.

2 large heads radicchio, leaves separated and torn into 1½-inch (4 cm) pieces

¼ cup (25 g) pecans

1 tablespoon pure maple syrup

Kosher salt

3 tablespoons extra-virgin olive oil

1½ tablespoons sherry vinegar

Freshly ground black pepper

1 small shallot, thinly sliced

1 ripe persimmon, preferably Fuyu, cored, halved, and thinly sliced

¼ cup (45 g) fresh pomegranate arils

Flaky sea salt

1. Submerge the radicchio in a large bowl filled with ice water. Let it soak for at least an hour and up to 2 hours to release some of its bitterness.

2. Line a rimmed half sheet pan with parchment paper. Cook the pecans in a small dry skillet over medium heat, stirring occasionally, until toasted and fragrant, 2 to 3 minutes. Remove from the heat, add the maple syrup (it will sputter and fizz), and gently toss until the pecans are coated. Sprinkle with a generous pinch of kosher salt and toss to combine. Quickly transfer the pecans to the prepared sheet pan, spaced apart, and let cool.

3. Whisk together the olive oil, vinegar, and a generous pinch of kosher salt and pepper in a small bowl. Stir in the shallot and let marinate while you assemble the salad, 5 to 10 minutes.

4. Drain the radicchio and pat dry, then transfer it to a serving bowl. Add the persimmon slices, drizzle with the vinaigrette, and gently toss to combine. Sprinkle with the pomegranate arils, maple pecans, and a pinch of flaky salt and serve.

Bunny Hill Blue Cheese Wedge

SERVES 4

For every ski town we love, there's a wood-paneled steak house we love just as much, and when this classic fork-and-knife salad hits the table—preferably after a cold gin martini—we feel the kind of unbridled glee that never goes out of style. Chill the dressing and the iceberg lettuce until just before serving for a classic salad that couldn't be simpler to get right.

DRESSING

¾ cup (180 ml) plain full-fat Greek-style yogurt

½ cup (120 ml) buttermilk

1 tablespoon Dijon mustard

1 tablespoon fresh lemon juice

½ teaspoon kosher salt

¼ teaspoon freshly ground black pepper

½ cup crumbled blue cheese (2 ounces/ 57 g)

SALAD

1 head iceberg lettuce, cut into 4 wedges

4 thick-cut bacon slices (8 ounces/ 225 g total), cut into ¼-inch-wide (6 mm) matchsticks and cooked until crisp

½ pint (110 g) cherry tomatoes, halved

1 tablespoon snipped fresh chives

Freshly ground black pepper

1. To make the dressing: Whisk together the yogurt, buttermilk, mustard, lemon juice, salt, and pepper in a small bowl. Stir in the blue cheese. Transfer to an 8-ounce (240 ml) mason jar. (If not using the dressing immediately, store it in the refrigerator for up to 3 days.)

2. To make the salad: Divvy up the iceberg wedges among four plates. Spoon the dressing on top of each wedge, taking care to drizzle some between the leaves. Sprinkle with the bacon, cherry tomatoes, chives, more dressing, and ground pepper, then serve.

Warm Cabbage and Butternut Squash Salad

SERVES 4

Sometimes compact cabbages can be hard to come by, so if you must buy a gargantuan one, use half; or double everything else and spread the salad between two sheet pans. If you aren't a big butternut squash fan, try delicata or acorn squash, or sweet potatoes (preferably orange ones, to preserve that beautiful purple-orange-green color combination). If you made a double batch of the chimichurri on page 114 and have plenty left over, use it in place of the cilantro dressing.

SALAD

1 small head red cabbage (about 1 pound/455 g), cut into ½-inch-wide (1.2 cm) wedges

1 small butternut squash (about 1 pound/455 g), peeled, halved lengthwise, seeded, and sliced into ½-inch-thick (1.2 cm) half-moons

1 bunch Broccolini

1 bunch scallions

1 red onion, cut into ½-inch-wide (1.2 cm) wedges

2 tablespoons extra-virgin olive oil

1 teaspoon kosher salt

½ teaspoon freshly ground black pepper

PEPITAS

¼ cup (35 g) hulled raw pepitas (pumpkin seeds)

½ teaspoon extra-virgin olive oil

¼ teaspoon red pepper flakes

⅛ teaspoon kosher salt

1. Preheat the oven to 425°F (220°C). Line a rimmed half sheet pan with parchment paper.

2. To make the salad: Toss the cabbage, squash, Broccolini, scallions, and all but one of the red onion wedges with the olive oil, salt, and black pepper. Arrange the vegetables evenly on the prepared sheet pan, then roast until tender and starting to caramelize, 25 to 30 minutes, tossing the vegetables once halfway through.

3. Meanwhile, to make the pepitas: Toast the pepitas in a small dry skillet over medium-high heat until puffy, crisp, and golden (some will pop), 2 to 3 minutes. Remove from the heat, let cool for a few minutes, then add the olive oil, red pepper flakes, and salt and toss to coat. Let cool completely.

4. To make the zesty onions: Zest the lime with a Microplane grater, then juice it (reserve the juice for the dressing). Cut the reserved red onion wedge into paper-thin slices, toss them with the lime zest and a big pinch of salt in a small bowl, and set aside.

5. To make the dressing: Combine the cilantro, garlic, lime juice, vinegar, salt, red pepper flakes, and black pepper in a food processor or blender and pulse to finely chop. With the motor running, add the olive oil in a thin stream and process until smooth. Transfer to a widemouthed 8-ounce (240 ml) mason jar. (The dressing can be stored in the refrigerator for up to

ZESTY ONIONS

1 lime
Kosher salt

CILANTRO DRESSING

2 cups packed (90 g)
    fresh cilantro,
    coarsely chopped
2 large garlic cloves
2 tablespoons fresh
    lime juice
1 teaspoon red wine
    vinegar
1 teaspoon kosher salt
½ teaspoon red pepper
    flakes
¼ teaspoon freshly
    ground black pepper
½ cup (120 ml) extra-
    virgin olive oil

2 ounces (57 g) feta
    cheese, crumbled
½ cup (20 g) fresh
    cilantro leaves
Flaky sea salt

AT THE CABIN

- Microplane grater
- Food processor or
  blender

3 days; let it sit out at room temperature for 20 to
30 minutes before serving to loosen it up.)

6. Arrange the roasted vegetables on a serving platter.
Drizzle the salad with half the dressing, then sprinkle
it with the zesty onions, feta, cilantro, pepitas, and a
generous pinch of flaky salt. Serve with the rest of the
dressing alongside.

Braised Greens with Feta, Preserved Lemon, and Chiles

SERVES 4

These good-for-you greens get their complexity from preserved lemon, a pantry staple that adds depth to the garlicky veg we crave in the winter. If you're already making your own preserved lemons, bravo! If not, look for preserved lemons online or in well-stocked grocery stores. This is a great dish to make for a large dinner, because it holds well at room temperature, but if it's just you, don't halve the recipe—the leftovers are delicious stirred into pasta or baked into a frittata (see the Tiny Tip).

1 preserved lemon
¼ cup (60 ml) extra-virgin olive oil
1 medium onion, thinly sliced
6 garlic cloves, smashed
2 bunches Tuscan (lacinato) kale, leaves stemmed and coarsely chopped
1 bunch broccoli rabe (or leafy green such as chard, escarole, or beet greens), chopped
½ cup (120 ml) white wine, broth, or water
Kosher salt and freshly ground black pepper
4 ounces (115 g) feta cheese, crumbled
1 to 2 Calabrian chiles in oil, sliced, oil reserved (optional)
Flaky sea salt

1. Slice the preserved lemon in half, remove and discard the pulp, and rinse the rind with water. Finely slice into ribbons.

2. Warm the olive oil in a Dutch oven over medium heat. Add the onion and cook, stirring often, for 10 to 12 minutes, until soft and beginning to brown. Add the garlic and cook for 2 minutes more, until fragrant.

3. Stir in the kale and broccoli rabe in batches, allowing each batch to wilt to make more room in the pot before adding the next. Stir in the wine and preserved lemon and cook, tossing with tongs, until the wine has evaporated and the stems of the broccoli rabe are tender, about 5 minutes. Remove from the heat.

4. Taste, season with kosher salt and pepper, and transfer to a serving platter. Top with the feta, Calabrian chiles and a drizzle of their oil (if you like things spicy), some pepper, and flaky salt. Serve immediately or at room temperature; it's equally delicious both ways.

TINY TIP: *For a Braised Greens Frittata, preheat the oven to 375°F (190°C). Whisk together 8 eggs and ¼ cup (60 ml) cream in a large bowl and stir in 2 cups (340 g) braised greens. Warm a short pour of olive oil in a skillet over medium heat. Add the egg mixture, give it a good stir, and sprinkle a little more feta on top. Bake for 12 to 20 minutes (baking time varies depending on the temperature of the ingredients and pan) until the eggs are set. Turn out onto a platter, slice into wedges, and serve.*

Fennel Flatbreads

MAKES 4

When your soup or salad needs a friend, put these easy fry breads on the side plates. Make them directly before serving, or make them ahead, then brush lightly with water and revive in a 450°F (230°C) oven for 2 minutes when ready to serve. They're delicious on their lonesome, or with olive oil, hummus, Red Pepper–Walnut Spread (page 48), or Ollie Ollie Onion Dip (page 50).

1 tablespoon fennel seeds
1 cup (130 g) spelt flour
1 cup (125 g) all-purpose flour, plus more for dusting
1 teaspoon baking powder
1 teaspoon kosher salt
¾ cup (180 ml) plain full-fat Greek-style yogurt
¼ cup (60 ml) milk
2 tablespoons extra-virgin olive oil
Grapeseed oil or other high-heat neutral oil, for frying

1. Toast the fennel seeds in a dry skillet over medium heat until fragrant, 2 to 3 minutes. Set aside to cool.

2. Stir together the spelt flour, all-purpose flour, toasted fennel seeds, baking powder, and salt in a large bowl until combined. Make a well in the center of the flour mixture; add the yogurt, milk, and olive oil; and mix until the dry ingredients are just incorporated. Cover the bowl with a damp kitchen towel and let rest for 10 minutes.

3. Turn out the dough onto a floured counter and cut it into 4 equal pieces. Sprinkle each piece with flour and roll into a ball with your hands, then roll out the dough with a rolling pin into rough ovals ¼ inch (6 mm) thick.

4. Heat a cast-iron skillet over medium-high heat for 2 to 3 minutes, until a sprinkle of water immediately sizzles when it hits the pan. Swirl a short pour (2 teaspoons or so) of grapeseed oil in the pan, then add one portion of the dough. Cook for about 2½ minutes on the first side, then flip and cook for 1½ minutes on the second side, until golden and beginning to puff. Tuck the flatbread into a basket lined with a kitchen towel to keep warm and repeat with the remaining dough, adding more oil to the pan as needed between batches. Serve immediately.

Fennel-Gorgonzola Gratin

SERVES 8 TO 10

A mandoline or a food processor fitted with a slicing disc makes quick work of slicing the potatoes for a gratin, allowing for swift assembly of the layers and keeping the potatoes from oxidizing to a sad gray hue. If you're working with a knife instead, transfer the sliced potatoes to cool water as you go to prevent discoloration, then drain them and pat dry before you assemble the dish.

1 garlic clove, halved lengthwise

1 tablespoon unsalted butter, for greasing

2½ cups (600 ml) heavy cream

3 ounces (85 g) Gorgonzola Dolce cheese

2 teaspoons kosher salt

1 teaspoon freshly ground black pepper

3 pounds (1.4 kg) Yukon Gold potatoes, scrubbed and thinly sliced (⅛ to ¼ inch/ 3 to 6 mm thick)

1 medium yellow onion, thinly sliced

3 cups (260 g) thinly sliced fennel (from 2 medium bulbs)

5 ounces (140 g) Gruyère, Comté, or Emmental cheese, grated

1. Preheat the oven to 350°F (180°C). Rub the cut sides of the garlic clove over the inside of a 9-inch (23 cm) oval gratin or baking dish. Butter the dish.

2. Bring the cream to a simmer in a small saucepan over low heat. Add the Gorgonzola and stir until melted. Strain the mixture through a fine-mesh sieve into a large liquid measuring cup.

3. Mix the salt and pepper in a small bowl. Spread one-third of the potatoes, onion, and fennel in the prepared baking dish. Sprinkle with one-third of the salt and pepper, then one-third of the Gruyère. Repeat to create three layers, finishing with the cheese.

4. Slowly pour the Gorgonzola cream into the dish. Bake for 1½ hours, or until the potatoes are tender and the top is crispy and browned. Let stand for at least 10 minutes before serving.

TINY TIP: *The gratin may be baked and stored in the refrigerator for up to 1 day before serving. When ready to serve, set it on the counter for 30 minutes to bring it to room temperature while the oven heats to 350°F (180°C). Cover the dish with aluminum foil and bake for 20 minutes until warmed through, then sprinkle extra shredded Gruyère on top and broil until melted and golden brown, about 3 minutes, before serving. Leftovers will keep for 3 days.*

MENU

SOUP NIGHT DELIGHT

A cozy plant-based menu for
Meatless Monday, Soup Sunday,
and any chilly day in between

Ollie Ollie Onion Dip   50
and Fennel Flatbreads   81

Roasted Kabocha Squash Soup   100

Root Vegetable, Red Chard,
Rosemary, and Rye Galette   112

Can't Catch Me Gingerbread Cakes
with Candied Kumquats   164

Cranberry-Cardamom Glogg   175

Grapefruit-Rosemary Spritzers   176

Butter Buns, Two Ways

MAKES 9

The bunny slope of buns, these soft, fluffy, downright irresistible dinner rolls are made with basic ingredients readily found in even the most scantily stocked rental cabin pantry (if the bread flour is elusive, use all-purpose instead), and can swing sweet or savory, depending on which butter you brush them with: Salted Honey or Garlic Rosemary. If you're baking for the entire ski class, double the recipe, and upgrade to a 12-inch (30 cm) skillet or a 9-by-13-inch (23 by 33 cm) baking dish.

BUNS

4 tablespoons
(½ stick/60 g)
unsalted butter,
plus more for greasing

2¼ cups (305 g) bread
flour, plus more for
dusting

3 tablespoons sugar

1¼ teaspoons kosher
salt

½ (¼-ounce/7 g) packet
active dry yeast
(1⅛ teaspoons)

3 tablespoons warm
water (110º to 115ºF/
43º to 46ºC)

½ cup (120 ml) whole
milk

1 large egg, beaten

1 egg, beaten with
1 tablespoon milk,
for egg wash

SALTED HONEY BUTTER

½ cup (1 stick/115 g)
unsalted butter,
at room temperature

¼ cup (60 ml) honey

1 teaspoon kosher salt

or

1. To make the buns: Butter a large bowl and set it aside. Stir together the flour, sugar, and salt in another large bowl. Combine the yeast and warm water in a small bowl and let sit until foamy, about 5 minutes.

2. Melt the butter in a small saucepan over low heat, then remove from the heat and stir in the milk (the mixture should be lukewarm; if it's too hot, let it cool a bit, or it may kill the yeast).

3. Add the egg, yeast mixture, and milk-butter mixture to the dry ingredients and mix until a shaggy, sticky dough forms.

4. Turn the dough out onto a lightly floured surface and knead it by hand, sprinkling with additional flour as needed (the dough will be sticky), until smooth and shiny, about 5 minutes. Transfer the dough to the greased bowl, cover with a kitchen towel, and let rise in a warm place until puffy and nearly doubled in size, about 2 hours.

5. Butter a 9-inch (30 cm) cast-iron skillet or an 8-inch (20 cm) square glass baking dish. Turn the dough out onto a lightly floured surface. Knead a few times, then divide the dough into 9 equal pieces (weigh them to be sure, if you're a perfectionist). Roll each piece into a ball, gently tucking the sides under several times to stretch the top smooth. Arrange the rolls in the prepared skillet or baking dish. (At this point, the rolls can be wrapped securely in plastic wrap and stored in the refrigerator for up to 2 days; or, freeze them on a parchment-lined baking sheet, transfer to an airtight container, and

GARLIC ROSEMARY BUTTER

½ cup (1 stick/115 g) unsalted butter, at room temperature
2 large garlic cloves, grated
1 tablespoon finely chopped fresh rosemary
¾ teaspoon kosher salt

store in the freezer for up to 1 month. When ready to bake, place the rolls in the buttered baking dish, and plan on a 3- to 4-hour rise in step 6.)

6. Cover the rolls loosely with a piece of lightly buttered plastic wrap and let them rest in a warm spot until puffy and nearly doubled in size, 1 to 1½ hours.

7. Preheat the oven to 350°F (180°C).

8. Uncover the rolls and brush the tops with the egg wash. Bake the rolls until deep golden brown, 20 to 23 minutes, depending on how squishy you like them.

9. Meanwhile, to make the compound butter: Combine all the ingredients in a small bowl (or in separate small bowls, if you're making both). Transfer to a widemouthed 8-ounce (240 ml) mason jar. (The butter can be made ahead and stored in the refrigerator for up to 3 days; let it sit out at room temperature for about 30 minutes before serving to soften it up.)

10. Remove the rolls from the oven and brush the tops with a bit of the compound butter. The rolls are best served warm (seriously, serve them warm), with the rest of the butter alongside. They will keep in an airtight container at room temperature for up to 3 days or in the freezer for up to 1 month. Before serving, sprinkle them with water, wrap them in aluminum foil, and rewarm in a preheated 350°F (180°C) oven until soft and squishy; about 10 minutes for room temperature, 15 to 20 minutes for frozen.

Classic Popovers

MAKES 6 POPOVERS

Will they? Won't they? The question of whether popovers will puff to perfection or fall flat keeps every cabin cook on the edge of their counter-height seat. Make your steam dreams come true by bringing the batter fully to room temperature (set it on the counter for at least 30 minutes) before pouring it into a piping-hot pan (see the Tiny Tips)—and, of course, exercising a stone-cold resolve not to open the oven while the popovers are baking.

1 cup (125 g)
   all-purpose flour
½ teaspoon kosher salt
2 large eggs
1 cup (240 ml) milk
6 teaspoons neutral
   oil, such as safflower
   or grapeseed

AT THE CABIN

- **Popover pan or muffin tin**

1. Set a popover pan on a sheet pan on the lowest rack of the oven. Move the other racks to the top positions and preheat the oven to 450°F (230°C).

2. Whisk together the flour and salt in a small bowl. In a separate bowl, whisk the eggs and milk for 1 minute, until frothy. Gradually whisk the flour into the wet ingredients until smooth. Transfer to a spouted container. (The batter can be covered and refrigerated overnight.)

3. Remove the pans from the oven and set them on a heat-safe surface. Measure 1 teaspoon of the oil into each well. Divide the batter evenly among the wells. Return the pans to the oven. Bake for 20 minutes, then reduce the oven temperature to 350°F (180°C) and bake for 10 minutes more until the popovers are puffed and golden, with crisp tops. (Resist the urge to open the oven and peek during baking! You could deflate the popovers and, in doing so, your ego.) Remove from the oven and invert the popover pan to remove the popovers (see Tiny Tips). Serve immediately.

TINY TIPS: *If you don't have a popover pan, a standard 12-cup muffin tin will do—just use only 10 wells, and measure ½ teaspoon oil into each.*

If you're not serving the popovers immediately, pierce each one with a paring knife to release steam. Turn off the oven, crack open the door with the handle of a wooden spoon, and let the popovers rest in the pan for up to 30 minutes.

Common Animal Snow Tracks

With a keen eye, this handy guide, and a little magical thinking, you'll soon become well versed in the age-old art of deciphering hibernal hints.

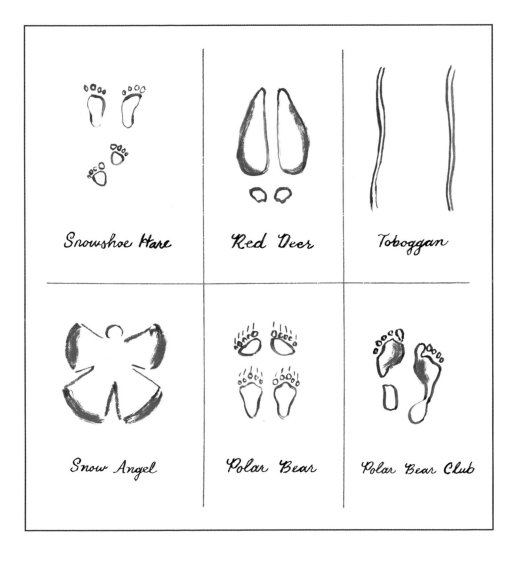

Snowshoe Hare	Red Deer	Toboggan
Snow Angel	Polar Bear	Polar Bear Club

How Have You Bean?
A Pantry Staple Primer

MAKES 3 CUPS (540 G)

Having beans on the scene makes improvising meals so much simpler. Serve beans with braised greens, stir them into soup, use them to top nachos and fill a burrito, or let them shine with just a swirl of chile oil or pesto and thick slices of grilled bread. If you're not yet on Team Bean, taste the heirloom varieties sold at farmers' markets or through online retailers like Rancho Gordo before deciding for good. Then follow this basic cooking method to prepare your pretties.

1 pound (455 g)
   dried beans
Olive oil
1 small onion,
   cut in half
1 bay leaf
2 teaspoons kosher
   salt

1. Spread the beans on a sheet pan and discard any that are shriveled or discolored, as well as any debris. Put the beans in a large bowl, cover with cool water by 2 inches (5 cm), and soak for at least 4 hours.

2. Drain the beans and transfer them to a heavy pot with a wide base. Add cool water to cover by 2 inches (5 cm), then add a glug of olive oil, the onion, and the bay leaf. Bring to a hard boil over medium-high heat, then boil for 10 minutes. Reduce the heat to low, cover the pot with the lid ajar, and simmer, adding more boiling water as needed to keep the beans submerged, until tender, about 2 hours. (The cooking time will vary based on the age of the beans.) Remove and discard the onion and bay leaf. Season the beans with salt and serve as is or upgrade as follows.

For Green Beans: Blanch 1 cup packed (about 50 g) assorted soft fresh herbs (basil, mint, cilantro, parsley) in boiling water for 10 seconds. Transfer to a bowl of ice and water, submerge briefly, drain, and pat dry. Place the blanched herbs in a food processor or blender, add ½ cup (120 ml) extra-virgin olive oil and ¼ teaspoon kosher salt, and process until smooth. Strain through a fine-mesh strainer. Drizzle the herb oil over the beans.

For Rosemary and Garlic Beans: Warm ¼ cup (60 ml) extra-virgin olive oil in a small skillet over medium heat and cook 3 minced garlic cloves and 1 teaspoon minced fresh rosemary until fragrant, about 2 minutes. Stir the mixture into the beans and simmer until the beans are warmed through.

Herb-Specked Spaetzle

SERVES 4

Whether you're an Austrian grandma, a home cook who misses one, or a dumpling dilettante, we assure you that although it's helpful to have a spaetzle grater, it's very possible to make spaetzle with nothing more than a cutting board, a knife, and your wits. (Consult the internet for impressive footage of grandmas speedily flicking their spaetzle into the pot, then take this at your own pace.) The rustic results will be well suited to short ribs, brisket, sheet-pan suppers, or even breakfast (sans parsley), swimming in a splash of maple syrup.

2 cups (250 g)
  all-purpose flour
6 large eggs, beaten
⅓ cup (80 ml) whole
  milk
Kosher salt
2 tablespoons
  unsalted butter
2 tablespoons neutral
  oil, such as safflower
  or grapeseed
¼ cup (13 g) minced
  fresh flat-leaf
  parsley

1. With a wooden spoon, vigorously stir together the flour, eggs, and milk in a large bowl until well combined and a little shiny. Cover and refrigerate for at least 30 minutes.

2. Bring a large pot of salted water to a boil. Fill a large bowl with ice and water.

3. Rinse a wooden cutting board with water so the spaetzle will slip off easily. Scoop a big spoonful of the batter onto the board. Dip an offset spatula or sharp knife into the boiling water and smooth the spoonful of dough over the board to reach the end. Holding the board over the water, use the edge of the spatula or knife to chop the dough into thin noodles and flick them off the board directly into the water; repeat until there's no dough left on the board. Cook until the spaetzle float to the top, 1 to 2 minutes, then use a skimmer to transfer them to the ice bath. Repeat with the remaining dough. (Working in batches like this prevents the early additions from overcooking.) Drain the spaetzle, spread them on a sheet pan, and pat dry with a paper towel.

4. Warm the butter and oil in a large skillet over medium-high heat. Add the spaetzle and cook, undisturbed, for 3 minutes, then flip them with a spatula and cook until crisp, turning every few minutes until crisp on both sides, about 10 minutes more. (Cooking time will vary based on how thinly you sliced the spaetzle.) Stir in the parsley, transfer to a serving bowl, and enjoy warm.

Coal-Baked Sweet Potatoes with Orange Whiskey Butter

SERVES 4

This compound butter adds a holiday-friendly upgrade to whatever yam is your jam—be it Jewels, Covingtons, or Japanese sweet potatoes. For the coziest cabin cooking, roast the potatoes over the coals in the fireplace, or tuck them in the woodstove. Serve with a bone-in pork chop, Brrrisket (page 132), or meatloaf. Spread leftover butter, which can be stored in the refrigerator for up to 2 weeks, on toasted challah, swirl into oatmeal, or stir into a hot buttered rum or mixed nuts (see the Tiny Tip).

4 medium sweet potatoes, scrubbed

½ cup (1 stick/115 g) unsalted butter, at room temperature

2 tablespoons dark brown sugar

1 tablespoon plus 1 teaspoon whiskey, such as Jack Daniel's (or Bulleit Bourbon, or whatever hooch the ski house is stocking)

2 teaspoons grated orange zest

1 teaspoon ground cinnamon

½ teaspoon ground ginger

½ teaspoon kosher salt

1. Prepare a fire in the woodstove or fireplace and let it burn down to hot coals, or preheat the oven to 425°F (220°C). Line a rimmed sheet pan with aluminum foil.

2. Prick the sweet potatoes all over with a paring knife. If using a woodstove or fireplace, wrap each potato in a double layer of foil and place the potatoes on the ledge inside the door of the woodstove or directly on the coals; if baking in the oven, place the potatoes on the prepared sheet pan. Bake for 45 minutes to 1 hour 15 minutes, depending on size (if using a woodstove or fireplace, rotate them frequently as they bake).

3. Meanwhile, use a fork to mash together the butter, brown sugar, whiskey, orange zest, cinnamon, ginger, and salt in a small bowl.

4. Use a paring knife to split the sweet potatoes lengthwise, and serve each topped generously with the whiskey butter.

TINY TIP: *For an outrageously good nut mix, toast 3 cups (420 g) mixed nuts (pecans are particularly good here) in a preheated 325°F (160°C) oven for 10 minutes until fragrant and one shade darker. Transfer the nuts to a bowl, stir in 2 tablespoons Orange Whiskey Butter, and serve warm.*

Brown Butter Brussels Sprouts, Parsnips, and Apples

SERVES 4

For the absolute best texture, corral any loose leaves from the Brussels sprouts into one area of the sheet pan before baking. After dressing the rest of the vegetables, sprinkle these crispy bits atop the dish.

2 pounds (910 g) Brussels sprouts, trimmed and halved

1½ pounds (680 g) parsnips (about 4), peeled, halved lengthwise, and cut into 2-inch-long (5 cm) segments

8 thyme sprigs

2 tablespoons extra-virgin olive oil

1½ teaspoons kosher salt

1 teaspoon freshly ground black pepper, plus more as needed

4 tablespoons (½ stick/60 g) unsalted butter

2 teaspoons Dijon mustard

1 tablespoon apple cider vinegar

1 small apple, cored and thinly sliced

Flaky sea salt

1. Position racks in the top and bottom thirds of the oven and preheat the oven to 425°F (220°C).

2. Combine the Brussels sprouts, parsnips, and 4 of the thyme sprigs in a large bowl. Drizzle with the olive oil, season with the kosher salt and pepper, and toss to combine. Divide between two sheet pans and roast for 20 minutes, turning midway through the cooking time with a metal spatula, until the Brussels sprouts are tender and their loose leaves are crispy and deeply browned, and the parsnips are fork-tender and starting to brown. Set the sheet pan on a wire rack while you make the dressing.

3. Melt the butter in a small, light-colored (so you can see the solids as they brown) saucepan over medium heat, swirling often. When the milk solids start to brown and the butter begins to smell like the best thing in the world, whisk in the mustard, then turn off the heat and add the vinegar. It will bubble vigorously.

4. Transfer the Brussels sprouts and parsnips to a bowl and add the apple slices. Pour the dressing over the top. Toss gently to coat, then season with flaky salt and pepper. Garnish with the remaining 4 thyme sprigs. Serve immediately.

TINY TIP: *In time, the acidic dressing will fade the Brussels sprouts to a sad, swampy hue, so resist the temptation to dress this dish in advance.*

Build a Better Snowperson

Bringing a snowperson into this world is no small responsibility, so here are a few tips on best building sites, how to ensure structural integrity, artful accessorizing, and why you should always be watching your back (collar).

Location, Location, Snowcation

Just like you'd rather have your ski cabin back up to a serene forest than a frenzied après-ski bar patio (unless you *like* getting splashed with Jägermeister while trying to relax on the back deck reading Mercer Mayer's nostalgic nail-biter, *Just a Snowman*), snowperson placement is key. Avoid the middle of the driveway, anywhere near the dryer vent or a natural hot spring, and right outside bedroom windows (lest you give someone who gets up for a midnight snack a serious night fright); instead, look for a nice flat stretch of fresh snow (shaded is helpful) with a little extra room in case you decide to grow your snow family (i.e., Calvin and Hobbes snow-army-style).

Grade A Snow DNA

Powder is perfect when you're laying down fresh tracks, wiping out, or trying to very hastily hide a treasure chest, but it's not ideal for forming oversize snowballs. Seek snow that's just wet enough to stick together without being slushy, and if this sort of snow is eluding you, either mist it with the hose to try to create the correct composition, or give up, go back inside, and watch *Olaf's Frozen Adventure* to see what could have been.

Tuck and Roll

You're eager to start rolling, but take the time to build a strong foundation first. Tightly pack a beach-ball-size snowball, then start spinning. When it's time to stack the head, snow-rax, and abdomen (best hummed to the chorus tune of the Banana Slug String Band's smash hit, "No Bones Within"), think layer-cake-style—firmly flatten the top of your base ball, set the second ball on top, and repeat with the head. This prevents a lopsided physique, and lowers the risk of your snowperson's noggin rolling into a ravine, which, in turn, lowers the risk of ear-piercing emotional meltdowns.

Cold Shoulder Scarf

Have the family fashionista creative-direct your snowperson's winter wardrobe, because while the old top hat, wool scarf, carrot, and coal combo is comfortingly classic, a modern Frosty deserves some flair—try a derby-worthy hat, rhinestone sunglasses, a bow tie and/or a feather boa, mittens or a faux-fur muff, twinkle lights, and a party horn (much healthier than a pipe). If everyone built their own snow buddy, stage your own (admittedly stationary) *Project Runway: The Mount Bachelor Meadow* version. Or, if the World Figure Skating Championships start in five minutes, your snowperson will look simply smashing in a top hat, wool scarf, carrot, and coal combo.

Watch Your Back

Sometimes, when one diligent individual is engrossed in building the best snowperson they can, another less scrupulous person will sneak up on them and stuff snow down the collar of their snow jacket. This is shocking and unsettling and can lead to an all-out snow brawl that accidentally, or not, destroys the hapless snowperson-in-progress. Keep a sharp eye out for shifty-looking co-snowperson creators, or, if that ship (snowball) has already sailed (down your back), return the favor by slipping a nice toasty handful of snow between the aggressor's sheets later that night, or by taping tiny pictures of infuriated abominable snowmen on the inside of their snow goggles.

Roasted Rainbow Carrots with Gremolata, Dill, and Toasted Walnuts

SERVES 4

A handful of fresh dill coupled with gremolata, that holy trinity of lemon zest, garlic, and parsley, gives these quick-roasted carrots formidable flavor. Look for bright, slender carrots, all roughly the same size so they roast evenly. If your carrots are particularly small, roast them whole so they don't get mushy. To make this a light plant-based main for two, thickly spread 1 cup (120 ml) of creamy hummus over the bottom of the platter and drizzle generously with olive oil before piling the carrots on top, then serve with plenty of warm, pillowy pita or a loaf of freshly baked bread for sopping everything up.

2 pounds (910 g) rainbow carrots (see Tiny Tip), with tops
1 tablespoon unsalted butter
2 tablespoons extra-virgin olive oil
1 teaspoon kosher salt
Freshly ground black pepper
¼ cup (30 g) coarsely chopped walnuts
1 lemon
1 large garlic clove, minced
¼ cup (13 g) finely chopped fresh flat-leaf parsley leaves
¼ cup (13 g) finely chopped fresh dill, plus ¼ cup (13 g) fresh dill fronds
Flaky sea salt

AT THE CABIN
• Microplane grater

1. Preheat the oven to 425°F (220°C). Line a rimmed half sheet pan with parchment paper.

2. Peel the carrots, if desired; trim the tops to 1 inch (2.5 cm); and halve each carrot lengthwise (or leave them whole if small).

3. Melt the butter in a small saucepan over medium-low heat, then add 1 tablespoon of the olive oil and swirl to combine. Spread the carrots evenly on the prepared sheet pan, drizzle with the warm butter and olive oil, sprinkle with ½ teaspoon of the kosher salt and a big pinch of pepper, and gently toss to combine. Bake the carrots until fork-tender and starting to caramelize, 20 to 25 minutes, tossing them once halfway through.

4. While the carrots are roasting, cook the walnuts in a small dry skillet over medium-low heat, tossing occasionally (don't let them burn), until toasted, 5 to 7 minutes. Set aside to cool slightly.

5. Zest the lemon into a small bowl with a Microplane grater; set the lemon aside for serving. Add the garlic, parsley, chopped dill, remaining ½ teaspoon kosher salt, and a big pinch of pepper and mix to combine. When the carrots are done roasting, remove them from the oven, sprinkle the lemon-dill mixture over the top, and very gently toss with two forks to combine.

6. Arrange the carrots on a serving platter or plate, drizzle the remaining 1 tablespoon olive oil (or more, if desired) over the top, and garnish with the toasted walnuts, dill fronds, and flaky salt. Cut the zested lemon into 8 wedges, arrange them around the platter, and serve.

TINY TIP: *The result won't be quite as comely, but you can swap the carrots for any root vegetable rolling around in the produce drawer or winter CSA box: parsnips, beets, turnips, kohlrabi, celery root, potatoes (both sweet and not)—just make sure to cut everything into roughly 1-inch (2.5 cm) pieces so it roasts evenly.*

CHAPTER 4

Mains

When it comes to dark and stormy night suppertime ambitions, sometimes you're ready to reach for Breckenridge's Peak 8 heights, and sometimes you're quite content to stay in the sno-park, so to speak. Whatever the evening's meal prep commitment level may be, this chapter has something sublime to stick in or on the stove, be it a melt-in-your-mouth Brrrisket with Parsley and Pomegranate or marvelously meatless Root Vegetable, Red Chard, Rosemary, and Rye Galette, simple and satisfying Chalet Cassoulet, a merry and memorable Ready, Set, Raclette feast, or any one of the savory sheet-pan suppers that promise one-pan dinner shazam without sacrificing an ounce of sophistication—not to mention keeping cabin kitchen cleanup to a minimum, so you have all the more time for a restorative pre-slumber sauna session (see Wanna Sauna? A Manners Manifesto for a quick sweat-iquette brushup).

Lemony Lentil Soup

MAKES ABOUT 8 CUPS (2 L)

This lemon-kissed lentil soup is a solid standby for those whirlwind winter days when you planned to make a twelve-layer lasagna for dinner but wore yourself out learning how to luge. Since curry powders are like snowflakes—no two are alike—get to know yours before you add it to the soup; if it's spicy, you may want to use less, and if it's not spicy enough, you might want to add a pinch of cayenne or splash of hot sauce.

LEMONY YOGURT TAHINI SAUCE

½ cup (120 ml) plain full-fat Greek-style yogurt
3 tablespoons extra-virgin olive oil
2 tablespoons tahini
Zest and juice of 1 lemon
1 small garlic clove, grated
¼ teaspoon kosher salt

LENTIL SOUP

4 tablespoons (60 ml) extra-virgin olive oil
1 medium yellow onion, diced (about 1 cup/110 g)
1 large kohlrabi or turnip, diced (about 1 cup/130 g)
3 celery stalks, diced (about 1 cup/100 g)
2 Yukon Gold potatoes, diced (about 1 cup/225 g)
1 teaspoon kosher salt, plus more for seasoning
6 large garlic cloves, grated (about 2 tablespoons)
2 tablespoons curry powder
1 (14.5 ounce/411 g) can crushed fire-roasted tomatoes

1. To make the yogurt sauce: Whisk together the yogurt, olive oil, tahini, lemon zest, lemon juice, garlic, salt, and ¼ cup warm water in a small bowl until smooth.

2. To make the soup: Heat 2 tablespoons of the olive oil in a large Dutch oven or stockpot over medium heat until shimmering. Add the onion, kohlrabi, celery, potatoes, and salt and cook until the onion is translucent and the vegetables are soft, 8 to 10 minutes. Add the garlic and cook until fragrant, about 30 seconds. Stir in the curry powder, then the tomatoes, and cook for about 1 minute. Stir in the lentils. Add 5 cups (1.2 L) of the broth and bring the soup to a boil.

3. Reduce the heat to maintain a simmer, cover, and cook, stirring occasionally, until the lentils are soft, 45 minutes to 1 hour (add more broth ½ cup/120 ml at a time if the soup seems too thick). At this point, take an immersion blender for a spin around the pot if you like your lentil soup on the creamier side (or transfer half the soup to a standing blender and purée it, then return it to the pot).

4. Stir in the chard and simmer the soup for 5 minutes more. Remove from the heat and stir in the lemon zest, lemon juice, and remaining 2 tablespoons olive oil. Season with salt and pepper to taste. Ladle the soup into bowls, drizzle with the yogurt sauce, sprinkle with the parsley, and serve.

- 1½ cups (300 g) French green lentils, rinsed
- 5 to 6 cups (1.2 to 1.5 L) vegetable broth
- 1 bunch chard, stems removed, leaves chopped into 1-inch (2.5 cm) pieces (about 4 cups/120 g; see Tiny Tips)
- Zest and juice of 1 lemon
- Freshly ground black pepper
- ¼ cup (13 g) chopped fresh parsley, for garnish

AT THE CABIN
- Immersion blender or blender (optional)

TINY TIPS: *If chard isn't in stock at the market, grab a bunch of fresh spinach or a 5-ounce (140 g) bag of baby spinach, or use half of a 16-ounce (455 g) bag of frozen spinach (if it's whole-leaf, chop it up before you toss it in the pot). If you happen to have a bunch of dill sitting around looking lonely, toss a big handful of chopped fresh dill in with the lemon and olive oil at the finish.*

If you'd like to speed things up in the lentils department, an hour before you begin to prep the soup, combine the lentils with 4 cups (1 L) of the vegetable broth and 1 teaspoon kosher salt in an Instant Pot, pressure cook on high for 12 minutes, and natural release.

Roasted Kabocha Squash Soup

SERVES 4

Roasting everything before blending it together gives this simple soup complexity, as does adding a swirl of cream and a sprinkling of chives and bacon before serving (if you're serving this on Meatless Monday or Vegan Tuesday, see the Tiny Tip). If you can't find kabocha—aka Japanese pumpkin, a rich, sweet, intensely orange Japanese winter squash—try a red kuri squash, butternut squash, or sugar pumpkin. If you have a smoker, smoking the squash in lieu of roasting it lends a divinely deep flavor. Serve the soup with thick slices of hot, melty cheddar or Gruyère toast (arrange the bread on a baking sheet, sprinkle with cheese, and broil for 1 minute), or gooey grilled cheese sandwiches.

1 (2- to 2½-pound/ 910 g to 1.1 kg) kabocha squash, halved and seeded
4 tablespoons (60 ml) extra-virgin olive oil
1 teaspoon kosher salt, plus more as needed
¼ teaspoon freshly ground black pepper, plus more as needed
1 yellow onion, cut into 8 wedges
1 large apple, peeled, cored, and cut into wedges
1 large shallot, quartered
4 slices thick-cut bacon
¼ teaspoon freshly grated nutmeg
2 cups (480 ml) vegetable broth
½ cup (120 ml) heavy cream
4 teaspoons minced fresh chives

AT THE CABIN
- **High-speed blender**

1. Preheat the oven to 400°F (200°C). Line a rimmed half sheet pan with parchment paper.

2. Brush the squash halves with 2 tablespoons of the olive oil, then sprinkle them liberally with salt and pepper. Place the halves cut-side down on one half of the prepared sheet pan. Combine the onion, apple, and shallot in a medium bowl, then toss with the remaining 2 tablespoons olive oil and a generous pinch each of salt and pepper; spread them on the other half of the sheet pan (set the bowl aside—no need to wash it).

3. Roast for 30 minutes, until the onion, apple, and shallot are soft and starting to caramelize. Pull the sheet pan out of the oven and use tongs to transfer them back to the bowl (if they aren't quite ready, keep them in for 5 to 10 minutes more); set aside. Turn the squash halves so they're cut-side up and roast until browned and very soft, 15 to 20 minutes more.

4. While the squash is roasting, cook the bacon in a large skillet over medium heat, turning occasionally, until just crispy, about 5 minutes. Use metal tongs to transfer the bacon to a paper towel–lined plate to drain and cool slightly. (Save the fat to cook fried eggs in.) When the bacon is cool enough to handle, chop or crumble it into ½-inch (1.2 cm) pieces.

5. When the squash is done roasting, remove it from the oven and let it sit on the pan until cool enough to handle. Scoop the flesh from the skin with a spoon (discard the skin) and place it in a high-speed blender. Add the roasted onion, apple, and shallot, the nutmeg, broth, salt, and pepper and purée until very smooth.

6. Transfer the soup to a Dutch oven or large saucepan and bring to a simmer over medium heat. Stir in the cream and remove from the heat. Add more salt and pepper, if desired. (If not serving immediately, let the soup cool, then transfer it to an airtight container and store in the refrigerator for up to 3 days or omit the cream and store in the freezer for up to 1 month.)

7. Divide the soup among four bowls. Garnish each with one-quarter of the bacon and 1 teaspoon of the chives, and serve.

TINY TIP: *To switch up this soup's flavor profile (and make it vegan), swap the heavy cream for coconut milk, the bacon for toasted pepitas (see page 78), and the chives for chopped cilantro.*

White Bean Chilly Chili with Tortilla Crisps

SERVES 6

Unless you're taking a cue from '90s ski fashion, in which case that one-piece neon ski suit is all the lewk you need, we're all about accessories. This speedy pressure-cooked chili is comforting on its own but comes alive with toppings, so go ahead and load up—the extras will find their way into nachos and Chilly-quiles Rojos (page 210). If you don't have an Instant Pot, see the Tiny Tip for Dutch oven instructions.

CHILI

2 pounds (910 g) boneless, skinless chicken thighs

2 teaspoons kosher salt, plus more if needed

1 teaspoon freshly ground black pepper

2 tablespoons extra-virgin olive oil

1 cup (180 g) diced poblano peppers (3 medium)

1 cup (180 g) diced white onion

1 tablespoon ground cumin

1 tablespoon dried Mexican oregano

2 teaspoons ground coriander

6 garlic cloves, minced

½ cup (90 g) finely diced jalapeños (2 large)

1 quart (1 L) chicken stock

3 cups (540 g) cooked white beans, such as cannellini, or 2 (15-ounce/425 g) cans, drained and rinsed

1. To make the chili: Season the chicken with 1 teaspoon of the salt and ½ teaspoon of the pepper.

2. Warm the olive oil in an Instant Pot on the sauté setting. Add the poblano peppers and onion and cook, stirring often to avoid browning, until tender, about 10 minutes. Combine the cumin, oregano, coriander, and remaining 1 teaspoon salt and ½ teaspoon pepper in a small bowl. Sprinkle the spice mix over the softened vegetables, stir in the garlic and jalapeño, and sauté for 1 minute, until fragrant. Add the stock, half the beans, and the chicken.

3. Lock on the lid and cook on high pressure for 15 minutes. Let the pressure release naturally for an additional 12 minutes, then quick release the additional pressure. Let cool for a few minutes, then gently shred the chicken inside the pot with two forks. Add the remaining beans to the Instant Pot.

4. To make the cilantro yogurt: Whisk together the yogurt, cilantro, lime juice, garlic, and salt in a small bowl.

5. To make the tortilla crisps: Heat 1 inch (2.5 cm) of grapeseed oil in a large skillet over medium-high heat until it shimmers. Fry the tortilla strips until golden brown, 30 seconds to 1 minute, turning them once (be careful not to underfry them or they won't be as crispy). Drain on paper towels.

CILANTRO YOGURT

1 cup (240 ml) plain full-fat Greek-style yogurt
3 tablespoons finely chopped fresh cilantro leaves
3 tablespoons fresh lime juice
1 small garlic clove, grated
⅛ teaspoon kosher salt

TORTILLA CRISPS

Grapeseed oil or other high-heat neutral oil, for frying
4 (6-inch/15 cm) corn tortillas, sliced in half and then into strips

TOPPINGS

Thinly sliced scallions, for serving
Freshly grated Monterey Jack cheese, for serving
Chopped fresh cilantro leaves, for serving

AT THE CABIN

- 6-quart Instant Pot

6. Scoop the chili into bowls and stir a spoonful of cilantro yogurt into each. Serve with scallions, grated cheese, cilantro, and the tortilla crisps.

TINY TIP: *If you're working with a Dutch oven rather than an Instant Pot, preheat the oven to 325°F (160°C) before getting started. In step 2, add all the beans at once. In step 3, cover the Dutch oven, transfer it to the oven, and cook for 2 hours.*

Cioppino Centoni

SERVES 6

One of our favorite cookbook authors/friends/people, the delightful, dynamic Danielle Centoni, riffed on her family's legendary recipe to get this divine version of cioppino, San Francisco's famous tomato-rich seafood stew. For this bona fide bleak-winter-night warmer, use any combination of seafood desired—if you can't find mussels, buy more clams instead, and if bass is on sale, swap it for the halibut. If Spanish chorizo isn't available, use a fully cooked, spicy sausage, such as andouille. Use fish stock, if you have it, or substitute 5 teaspoons of a concentrated lobster base (such as Better Than Bouillon), dissolved in 4 cups (1 L) water.

2 teaspoons fennel seeds

2 tablespoons extra-virgin olive oil

½ pound (225 g) dry-cured Spanish chorizo, diced

1 large onion, diced

3 tablespoons tomato paste

4 garlic cloves, minced

1 cup (240 ml) dry white wine

4 cups (1 L) fish stock

8 ounces (240 ml) clam juice

1 (28-ounce/795 g) can whole plum tomatoes

2 teaspoons kosher salt

1 teaspoon freshly ground black pepper

1 teaspoon red pepper flakes (optional)

½ teaspoon ground allspice

¼ cup (13 g) chopped fresh flat-leaf parsley

2 bay leaves

1 pound (455 g) clams, scrubbed (see Tiny Tip)

1. Place a large Dutch oven or stockpot over medium-high heat. Add the fennel seeds and toast, stirring occasionally, until fragrant and beginning to color, about 2 minutes. Remove from the heat, transfer to a spice grinder or mortar and pestle, and grind to a powder.

2. Return the pot to the heat and add the olive oil. Add the diced chorizo and sauté until the fat renders and it begins to brown, about 5 minutes. Add the onion and sauté until translucent. Push the onion and chorizo to one side of the pot and add the tomato paste. Cook the paste until it begins to darken, about 2 minutes, then stir it into the onion and chorizo. Add the garlic and cook for 1 minute more.

3. Add the wine and stir to deglaze the pan, scraping up all the browned bits from the bottom. Pour in the stock and clam juice. Add the whole tomatoes, crushing each with your hand as you add it to the pot, along with their juices. Add the ground toasted fennel, salt, black pepper, red pepper flakes (if using), allspice, parsley, and bay leaves. Cover, bring to a boil over high heat, then reduce the heat to maintain a simmer. Simmer gently for 30 minutes. (The cioppino base can be made a day ahead; let it cool, then transfer it to an airtight container and store in the refrigerator.)

1 pound (455 g)
  mussels, scrubbed
  and debearded
  (see Tiny Tip)
4 ounces (115 g)
  calamari rings and
  tentacles
1 pound (455 g) firm
  white-fleshed fish,
  such as halibut or
  cod, cut into large
  chunks
8 ounces (115 g)
  raw extra-jumbo
  (16/20-count)
  shrimp, peeled and
  deveined
1 (2-to 3-pound/910 g
  to 1.4 kg) cooked
  and cleaned
  Dungeness crab,
  legs removed and
  cracked, body
  quartered

AT THE CABIN
- Mortar and pestle
- Seafood crackers

4. Just before serving, bring the base to a strong simmer over medium-high heat. Add the clams and mussels and cover the pot. Simmer until their shells have begun to open, about 5 minutes. Add the calamari, fish, and shrimp and simmer until each is opaque throughout, about 5 minutes. Add the crab legs and body and cook to heat through, about 2 minutes. Remove from the heat and discard any clams or mussels that haven't opened.

5. Divide the cioppino among six bowls and serve with crusty bread and a simple green salad.

TINY TIP: *If your clams are wild, not farmed, soak them in water to cover for 30 minutes to 1 hour, which helps them spit out their sand. Hopefully, your mussels came debearded; if not, grab on to the whiskery strands peeking out from between the shells and pull until they come off. Toss any clams or mussels that have chipped shells or are gaping open and refuse to shut if you tap their shell, and after cooking, discard any that haven't opened.*

Mussels with Coconut Milk, Ginger, and Lemongrass

SERVES 4

Dishing up wide bowls of steaming mussels is one of our favorite ways to make dinner for a group. The meal comes together so quickly that no one has to leave the conversation to cook, and it cleans up equally fast, so there's plenty of time for a round of games afterward. To save even more time, make the broth ahead (it will keep in the refrigerator for up to a week), then bring it to a simmer before adding the mussels.

4 pounds (1.8 kg) mussels
2 tablespoons coconut oil or neutral oil, such as safflower or grapeseed
1 cup (55 g) thinly sliced scallions (from 2 bunches)
2 teaspoons grated fresh ginger (grated on a Microplane)
4 garlic cloves, minced
½ serrano pepper, seeded
1 lemongrass stalk, tough outer layers removed, tender portion coarsely chopped
1 cup (240 ml) dry white wine
1 (13.5-ounce/385 g) can unsweetened coconut milk
1 teaspoon fish sauce
½ cup (20 g) coarsely chopped fresh cilantro, plus sprigs to garnish
Lime wedges, for serving
Crusty bread, for serving

AT THE CABIN
- Microplane grater

1. Rinse the mussels in cold water; scrub off any lingering visible dirt and use a paring knife to pull off any remaining beards from the mussels. If your mussels are wild, soak them in water for 30 minutes to 1 hour, which helps them spit out any sand (see Tiny Tip).

2. Melt the coconut oil in a Dutch oven over medium heat. Add the scallions and cook, stirring frequently, until softened but not browned, 3 minutes. Add the ginger, garlic, and serrano pepper and cook for an additional minute. Add the lemongrass, wine, coconut milk, and fish sauce and bring to a gentle simmer.

3. Add the mussels and cover the pot. Cook, shaking the pot now and then, until all the shells have opened, about 8 minutes. (If a few stubborn ones remain closed, cook for another minute. If any still remain shut after that, discard them.) Turn off the heat and stir in the chopped cilantro.

4. Ladle into wide bowls, garnish with cilantro sprigs, and serve with lime wedges and slabs of warm bread for dipping. Set a bowl in the middle of the table for empty shells.

TINY TIP: *Wild mussels are grand, but know that farm-cultivated mussels are a sustainable choice—plus, they have the added benefit of being already cleaned and purged of sand. For the most magnificent moules, look for shells that are tightly closed (or just slightly agape) and wet on the outside. At home, transfer the mussels to a bowl, cover with a damp kitchen towel, and store in the refrigerator for up to 2 days before steaming.*

Bowled Over

The premise of a bread bowl is simple: Why eat your soup *with* your bread when you can eat your soup *in* your bread? It was the question on civilization's mind as early as medieval times, when the first doughy dish was served to impress a British duke in 1427. But it wasn't until the 1980s that the roll bowl truly took off, thanks to a San Francisco craze for sourdough boules filled with clam chowder. A few years ago, in an innovation we're still pondering, Panera Bread moved the needle by rolling out the *double* bread bowl, allowing not one but *two* soups to be served in side-by-side kitschy, clever, and downright carb-y hollows. (Minds were blown.) If you wish to bring the bread bowl back to your winter table, cabin time might be the right time. If, however, you're not yet ready to commit to eating an entire-ish loaf of bread, a decadent and yet somehow more reasonable alternative is to float slices or torn pieces of bread atop the soup to cover the surface of the Dutch oven, sprinkle the top with shredded Parmesan, and bake in a preheated 425°F (220°C) oven for 10 minutes, or until golden brown.

Soup, There It Is

If there's one culinary tenet we stand by, it's the steadfast belief that chocolate cures all. But if there are two, it's that having a pot of soup on hand is the key to healthfully surviving hibernation season. After the first cold snap, we break out the Dutch oven every Sunday to make a soup that will carry us through the week. If you, too, have soup goals, keep these tips and tricks in mind.

Extras, Extras

Maximize your vegetables, save money for your chocolate allowance, and reduce food waste by making your own vegetable stock. Keep a gallon-size (4 L) bag in the freezer in which to store all your leftover bits and bobs—the base of the celery bunch, ends of onions, tops of parsnips and carrots, shriveled ginger, parsley stems, thyme past its prime—and when the bag is full, combine the goods in the largest pot you own with a teaspoon of whole black peppercorns and a bay leaf, and cover with water by 2 inches (5 cm). Bring to a boil, then simmer, uncovered, for 4 hours, skimming off any foam that rises to the surface. Strain through a fine-mesh strainer and pour into quart (liter) containers. Let cool, then refrigerate for up to 3 days or freeze for up to 6 months. (In a separate freezer bag, freeze your Parmesan rinds to toss into vegetable soups that need some oomph.)

Now and Later

Soup may be famous for its cold storage qualifications, but not all recipes are freezer-ready equal. Thick stews, such as chili and braises, do superbly well. Broth-based soups can be equally spectacular but freeze best without their starchy stir-ins: noodles, potatoes, and rice. Omit these before freezing and leave a note for your future self that you did, so you'll remember to add them later. This is also a good practice for cream, which can separate after freezing, and fresh herbs and greens, which will lose their good looks.

Freeze Tag

Cool the soup to room temperature before transferring it to resealable containers, leave 1 to 2 inches (2.5 to 5 cm) at the top for soup expansion (for a mason jar, stay under the threads), and, of course, be certain to label all containers, not only so you don't accidentally defrost chicken chili on Meatless Monday but also to remember to eat the contents within 3 months.

Time for a Warm-Up

Defrost the soup in its container overnight in the refrigerator or set the container in a bowl of warm water until the soup easily releases. Transfer the soup to a pot; slowly reheat over low heat, adding more broth or water if necessary (or any omitted ingredients); and adjust the seasoning before serving.

MENU

READY, SET, RACLETTE

**The more melted cheese,
the merrier, we always say.**

**Chestnuts Roasting
in a Closed Oven   39**

**Radicchio, Persimmon,
and Maple Pecan Salad   76**

Raclette   110

**Burnt Honey and
Thyme Roasted Pears   162**

Bottles of chilled saison

Dry Riesling

Calvados Hot Toddies   185

Perfect Your Raclette Etiquette

If your favorite winter mealtime motto is "melted cheese, and lots of it," it's time to plot a rousing Riesling-splashed raclette night. It's surprisingly straightforward; the only specialized skill required is the ability to slice cheese (and if you're lucky, the cheesemonger will do that for you), most ingredients can be found at even the sparsest supermarkets, and any leftovers make a mean scramble or hash the next morning. Here are a few party principles to help you pull off the ultimate raclette fête.

Hey, Party Grill

Traditional raclette machines involve hoisting a half wheel of raclette cheese into a metal arm that suspends it at a slant with the cut side exposed to heat, prompting the cheese to melt and cascade in great, gooey waves over whatever you're holding beneath it—boiled potatoes, baguette, cupped hands. A less expensive and easy-to-transport tabletop version, or raclonette, sports a double-decker design with a griddlelike upper tier for searing sausage and grilling vegetables and a lower level that holds and heats up to eight sturdy nonstick paddles, aka coupelles, perfect for melting slices of cheese, then pouring them over meat, vegetables, bread, and everything else in sight. (See Pantry Provisions on page 218 for raclette grill recommendations.)

Ready, Set, Raclette

When prepping for your melted cheese melee, plan on roughly 8 ounces (225 g) raclette cheese per person. It should be readily available at your favorite neighborhood fromagerie, specialty market, or online cheese shop. No raclette? Don't fret: substitute something comparably mild and melty, such as fontina, Havarti, Gouda, Gruyère, or Emmental (in case you were agonizing over what to name your new quintet of Saint Bernard puppies, you're welcome).

Rally the Raclette Troops

Slice the cheese about ⅛ inch (3 mm) thick, pile sliced baguettes and soft pretzel braids (see page 54) on a platter, and assemble the fixings—traditional raclette accoutrements include boiled potatoes, cornichons, pickled onions, and mustard, but feel free to improvise with sliced ham, prosciutto, salami, sausage, hard-boiled eggs, raw and roasted vegetables, wild mushrooms, assorted pickles, fresh fruit and herbs, and sauces, such as aioli and pesto.

The More, the Meatier

Those who have disavowed dairy need not sit at the sad table; if there are Paleos present, prepare a platter of sliced skirt steak, salmon, shrimp, and bacon-wrapped asparagus for grilling. For vegans, stock up on plant-based cheese with suitable meltability, sliced tofu, and plenty of vegetables (to avoid cross contamination, you may want to invest in a dedicated meat-free raclette set, especially if you're a dual-diet family).

Dessert Dips

Most raclette grills have a reversible cook plate, with one ridged side for grilling and one smooth side for Nutella-crepe-making (or something like that). After supper, flip the savory side over and cook crepes on the sweet side, filling them with fresh fruit, jam, Tangerine Dream Curd (page 153), and the chocolate or Nutella you've been melting/warming in your handy paddles. Fold, dollop generously with whipped cream, dust with nuts and sprinkles, and devour. Alternatively, use the paddles to broil marshmallows and melt chocolate squares atop graham cracker squares, then smoosh them together. Voilà—flame-free s'mores.

Clink and Drink

Rich and decadent raclette calls for a crisp, dry white wine, like a Riesling, Grüner Veltliner, or Roussette de Savoie; or if you prefer red wine, a Côtes du Rhône, gamay, or pinot noir. Beer drinkers, try a light pilsner or Belgian ale. After dinner? Mandatory shots of kirsch, a bracing cherry brandy and traditional digestif. There's really only one ironclad rule of raclette refreshments: no water (unless it's in hot tea). The Swiss believe it makes the cheese seize, leading to a disgruntled digestive system, and we're not going to argue with the keen minds behind Velcro, aluminum foil, muesli, and, of course, the Swiss Army knife (an excellent pinch hitter in the event that you've misplaced the cheese slicer).

Let's Spoon

Should a power outage put your electric raclette grill out of commission, build a fire, set out the cheese and accoutrements along the hearth, pour the wine, pass out long-handled metal spoons to serve as improvised live-fire coupelles, and proceed as planned. (In case you forgot, the plan is: pour melted cheese and chocolate on everything in sight, except maybe the cat.)

Root Vegetable, Red Chard, Rosemary, and Rye Galette

SERVES 6

Use a vegetable peeler to slice the parsnips for this easy savory galette, and a mandoline to cut the potatoes; the thinner they are, the more tender they'll be. Any variety of chard will do, but we like red for its bold crimson stems. Serve the galette with a simple green salad for a meat-free main; or, for a hearty post-bobsledding snack, cut it into smaller pieces and serve with a crisp white wine. If eating leftovers for breakfast, pop a crispy-edged fried egg on top.

CRUST

1½ cups (190 g) all-purpose flour
½ cup (50 g) rye flour
¾ teaspoon kosher salt
¾ cup (1½ sticks/170 g) cold unsalted butter, cut into cubes
4 to 6 tablespoons (60 to 90 ml) ice water

1. To make the crust: Whisk together the all-purpose flour, rye flour, and salt in a medium bowl. Add the butter and work it into the flour mixture with your hands (pretend you're snapping your fingers together) until coarse crumbs form. Add the ice water 2 tablespoons at a time, working it in with your hands, until a crumbly dough forms (when you pinch it with your fingers, it should hold together). Press the dough into a 1-inch-thick (2.5 cm) rectangle, wrap it in plastic wrap, and refrigerate for at least 30 minutes and up to 3 days (remove from the refrigerator and let soften for 15 minutes or so before rolling it out).

2. While the dough is chilling, make the filling: Set a fine-mesh sieve over a bowl. Place the ricotta in the sieve and set aside to drain.

3. Heat the olive oil in a Dutch oven or large skillet over medium heat until shimmering. Add the shallots and garlic and cook until fragrant, about 30 seconds. Add the chard and cook until soft, about 5 minutes. Season with ¼ teaspoon of the salt and a pinch of pepper. (If you use a skillet, the chard will overfill it, so add some and let it wilt before adding the remainder; covering the skillet will help the chard wilt faster.)

4. Preheat the oven to 400°F (200°C).

FILLING

1 cup (240 ml) whole-milk ricotta cheese

2 tablespoons extra-virgin olive oil

2 large shallots, minced (about ½ cup/70 g)

3 large garlic cloves, minced

2 bunches red chard, chopped (about 8 cups/440 g)

½ teaspoon kosher salt

Freshly ground black pepper

3 teaspoons minced fresh rosemary

½ pound (225 g) parsnips, sliced paper thin

1 cup (110 g) grated Gruyère cheese (about 4 ounces)

3 Yukon Gold potatoes (about ¾ pound/ 340 g), sliced paper thin

1 egg, beaten with 1 tablespoon milk, for egg wash

AT THE CABIN

- Mandoline

5. Remove the dough from the refrigerator and roll it out on parchment paper into a 16-by-12-inch (40.5 by 30 cm) rectangle, lightly dusting with flour as necessary to keep the rolling pin from sticking. Transfer the dough on the parchment to a rimmed quarter or half sheet pan.

6. Transfer the drained ricotta to a small bowl, mix in the remaining ¼ teaspoon salt and a pinch of pepper, and spread the ricotta over the dough, leaving a roughly 2-inch (5 cm) border. Sprinkle with 1 teaspoon of the rosemary. Layer the parsnips evenly on top, then sprinkle with ⅓ cup (35 g) of the Gruyère and 1 teaspoon of the rosemary. Next, layer on the potatoes, ⅓ cup (35 g) of the Gruyère, and the remaining 1 teaspoon rosemary. Spread the chard over the top and sprinkle with the remaining ⅓ cup (35 g) Gruyère. Carefully fold the edges of the dough over the filling to create a roughly 1½-inch (4 cm) border.

7. Gently patch up any cracks in the crust, and thoroughly brush the exposed dough with the egg wash. Bake the galette until the filling is bubbling and the crust is golden brown, 50 to 55 minutes. Remove the galette from the oven, let cool for 5 to 10 minutes in the pan, cut into squares, and serve.

TINY TIP: *Meat lovers, fry up 4 to 8 ounces (115 to 225 g) of bacon, or save a few slices from breakfast (see Tiny Tips on page 200), and sprinkle crispy bacon bits into the galette's layers.*

Cauliflower Steaks with Smoky Yogurt and Chimichurri

SERVES 4

Should the winter farmers' market have green, purple, or orange cauliflower, grab a variety of colors; the contrast will be striking (in a good way, not a lightning-bolt-to-the-cabin-satellite-dish kinda way).

CHIMICHURRI

2 cups (about 75 g) packed coarsely chopped flat-leaf parsley
⅓ cup fresh or 1½ teaspoons dried oregano
3 garlic cloves
1 teaspoon kosher salt
½ teaspoon red pepper flakes
½ teaspoon freshly ground black pepper
3 tablespoons red wine vinegar
1 tablespoon fresh lemon juice
1 cup (240 ml) extra-virgin olive oil

2 medium heads of cauliflower (about 2 pounds/ 910 g each), leaves removed
Extra-virgin olive oil, for brushing
Kosher salt and freshly ground black pepper

QUINOA

2 cups (375 g) tricolor quinoa
3 cups (720 ml) vegetable broth
2 tablespoons extra-virgin olive oil
¾ teaspoon kosher salt

1. To make the chimichurri: Combine the parsley, oregano, garlic, salt, red pepper flakes, and black pepper in a food processor and process until very finely chopped. Transfer to a small bowl and stir in the vinegar, lemon juice, and olive oil. (The chimichurri can be stored in the refrigerator for up to 5 days; let it sit out at room temperature for 20 to 30 minutes before serving to loosen up.) Set aside to let the flavors deepen.

2. Position racks in the top and bottom thirds of the oven and preheat the oven to 425°F (220°C). Line two rimmed half sheet pans with parchment paper.

3. Trim the stem of each cauliflower flat, then sit the whole head (stem-side down) on a cutting board and carefully cut it lengthwise into 1-inch-thick (2.5 cm) slices (use a very sharp knife or a bread knife). You should get two or three full "steaks" out of each head of cauliflower; the ends and crumbly bits won't be quite as picturesque but will be just as delicious, so roast them along with the steaks.

4. Divide the cauliflower steaks between the prepared sheet pans. Brush one side of each steak with olive oil and sprinkle generously with salt and pepper, then flip and repeat on the other side. Roast until tender and starting to brown, about 20 minutes per side, flipping the steaks and rotating the pans halfway through.

5. While the cauliflower is cooking, make the quinoa and smoky yogurt: Place the quinoa in a fine-mesh strainer, rinse well under cold running water, and drain. Stir together the quinoa, broth, olive oil, and salt in a 3-quart (3L) saucepan. Bring to a boil over medium-high

SMOKY YOGURT

- **1 cup (240 ml) plain full-fat Greek-style yogurt**
- **1 tablespoon extra-virgin olive oil**
- **1 tablespoon fresh lemon juice**
- **1 small garlic clove, grated**
- **½ teaspoon smoked paprika**
- **¼ teaspoon smoked sea salt**

AT THE CABIN

- **Food processor**
- **Fine-mesh strainer**

heat, reduce the heat, cover, and simmer for 20 minutes, then let rest with the lid on for 10 minutes. Fluff with a fork before serving.

6. To make the smoky yogurt: Whisk together the yogurt, olive oil, lemon juice, garlic, paprika, and salt in a small bowl.

7. When the cauliflower is finished roasting, remove it from the oven and let it cool for a few minutes. Stir together the quinoa and 1 cup (240 g) of the chimichurri, then transfer the quinoa to a large serving platter and arrange the cauliflower on top. Spoon the remaining chimichurri over the cauliflower and serve the smoky yogurt alongside.

TINY TIP: *Got leftover cauliflower? Lucky you! Fold it into an omelet, rewarm it and drizzle with leftover chimichurri or Lemony Yogurt Tahini Sauce (see page 98), stuff it into tacos, or sauté it with greens and serve over beans.*

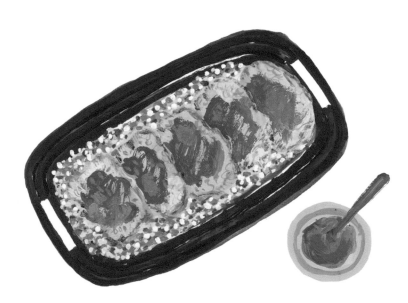

Much Ado About Dumplings

Make the best of a dark and snowy night by gathering the gang around the cabin table for a lively interactive evening of DIY dumplings.

Wrap It Up

Gather provisions ahead of time, starting with a stack of 3½-inch (9 cm) round dumpling "skins," aka wrappers; we like Japanese gyoza wrappers for their delicate, not-too-doughy nature, which lets the fillings shine. (Gyoza are the Japanese adaptation of Chinese jiaozi, or dumplings.) Find them in the grocery store's refrigerated or frozen section, or at an Asian market, and buy more than you think you'll need, as they're an inexpensive and invaluable freezer staple.

To Be, or Not to Be . . . Meaty

If your crew skews plant-based, mix up an equally appetizing vegetarian or vegan filling by replacing meat with tofu, edamame, cabbage, carrots, and/ or mushrooms (sauté them until soft before incorporating). Double-check the ingredients list for store-bought wrappers; most are vegan, but some contain egg. You can also roll your own wrappers if you have the time, flour, salt, water, and patience.

Gyoza Gang

The "many hands make light work" proverb has never been truer than now; folding a family-size batch of dumplings solo can take a while, so unless you need the quiet time/finger workout, this is a prime opportunity to recruit kitchen collaborators. See page 118 for how to set up dumpling-stuffing stations.

Sticky Situation

A dumpling's second favorite thing in life (besides being pinched) is to stick to the pan, so as much as you love your stainless-steel and cast-iron skillets, in this case, nonstick reigns supreme. A 10-inch (25 cm) nonstick skillet will accommodate about a dozen dumplings at a time, so fire up two, or, preferably, break your extra-large lidded electric skillet out of the basement and fry up entire batches at once. (Wanna steam/simmer instead? See the cooking instructions on page 119.)

Portion Control (or Lack Thereof)

One of the most important principles of potsticker production is to wildly overestimate how many your group will gobble up, because they freeze beautifully, and few things are as exciting to find while randomly rifling through the freezer. Plan on six to eight dumplings per light eater, a dozen per medium eater, and two dozen per restraint-resistant eater. Put the resulting overage on ice: arrange the dumplings in a single layer (not touching) on a parchment-lined sheet pan, freeze them until firm (about 30 minutes), transfer them to resealable freezer bags labeled by flavor, and freeze for up to 1 month.

We Have Fillings for You

EACH RECIPE MAKES ENOUGH FILLING FOR ABOUT 50 DUMPLINGS

These recipes will get you started on your dumpling-devouring journey, but feel free to improvise. It doesn't take much to make a divine dumpling—a handful of ground meat or minced mushrooms, a variety of vegetables, scallions galore, a little/lotta garlic here, a little/lotta ginger there (we lean toward a lotta). And you'll need 50 gyoza wrappers to assemble the dumplings.

PORK GINGER SCALLION

1 pound (455 g) ground pork
½ pound (225 g) finely chopped or grated green cabbage (about 3 cups; toss with 1 tablespoon kosher salt, let sit for 15 minutes, then gently squeeze dry)
½ cup (30 g) thinly sliced scallions
2 tablespoons grated fresh ginger
1 tablespoon grated garlic
1 tablespoon soy sauce
1 teaspoon toasted sesame oil

Mix all the filling ingredients in a large bowl with a spatula or your hands. Fill and fold 50 gyoza wrappers as instructed on page 118, and see page 119 for cooking instructions. Serve with dipping sauce (recipe follows). If you're not eating the dumplings right away, freeze them, uncooked (see opposite for instructions).

SHIITAKE SAKE

1 pound (455 g) shiitake mushrooms, finely chopped (sauté with 2 tablespoons neutral oil, 1 teaspoon kosher salt, and 2 tablespoons sake until soft and the liquid has evaporated)
5 ounces (140 g) finely chopped spinach (about 2 cups)
½ cup (30 g) thinly sliced scallions
½ cup (50 g) packed finely chopped cilantro, leaves and stems
1 tablespoon sake
2 teaspoons grated fresh ginger
2 teaspoons grated garlic
1 teaspoon kosher salt

DIPPING SAUCE

¼ cup (60 ml) soy sauce
2 tablespoons rice vinegar
1 tablespoon thinly sliced scallions
1 teaspoon sesame seeds
1 teaspoon toasted sesame oil
1 teaspoon chile oil (optional)

Mix all the ingredients in a small bowl and serve.

Pleat and Eat: A Dumpling Pictorial

Before there is eating, there must be pleating, and in this case, practice really does make perfect. The technique is simple but can be tricky to master; fortunately, even homely dumplings taste terrific. So prep your production line, and start stuffing!

1. Set up a station for each person, with a sheet pan (or cutting board), spoon, small bowl of water, wet washcloth for wiping messy fingers, and stack of dumpling wrappers. (Set the bowls of premade filling and a sheet pan to collect the finished dumplings in the middle.)

2. Spoon a scant tablespoon of filling into the center of each wrapper. Dip a finger in water and run it around the edge of the wrapper.

3. Fold the wrapper in half and use your thumbs and forefinger to pleat and pinch the two sides shut (aim for five or six pleats). Alternate method: Pinch (haphazardly) and pray (that the dough holds).

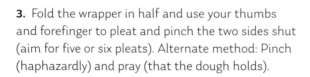

4. Set the finished dumpling on the sheet pan. Repeat. (Keep your wrappers covered with a damp dish towel while you work, so they don't dry out.)

5. Wash your hands well, especially if raw meat was involved, then congratulate the group on their dazzling dumpling-making endeavors. Optional prizes to be awarded: (Aesthetics) Flawless Folder Extraordinaire, (Output) Most Productive Pleater, (Attitude) Least Whiny Worker.

How to Cook a Dumpling

There's more than one way to cook a dumpling, so whether you're #panfriedforlife, on an all-soup diet, or have been dying to fire up the new electric deep fryer Santa delivered, you're covered.

Panfry

Heat 1 to 2 tablespoons of vegetable or canola oil in a 10-inch (25 cm) lidded nonstick skillet over medium-high heat until hot but not smoking. Add about a dozen dumplings and fry until the bottoms are brown (golden brown, not soy sauce brown), 2 to 3 minutes. Add ½ cup (120 ml) water, cover the skillet, and cook until the water has evaporated and the dumplings are cooked through, 4 to 6 minutes. (Cut a dumpling open to double-check doneness.) Remove the lid, give the skillet a good shake to loosen the dumplings, and let the bottoms re-crisp, 1 to 2 minutes.

Steam

Line a bamboo or stainless-steel steamer with parchment paper. Add the dumplings and steam, covered, until cooked through, about 10 minutes.

TINY TIP: *To cook frozen dumplings, apply these same methods, but add a few minutes—and when in doubt, cut a dumpling open and check it out.*

Boil

Boil the dumplings in water, stock, or noodle soup until cooked through, 5 to 7 minutes.

Deep-Fry

Heat about 2 inches (5 cm) of vegetable or canola oil to 350°F (180°C) in a deep pot or Dutch oven (or use the aforementioned electric deep fryer). Add the dumplings (don't crowd them—even potstickers need their personal space) and fry until golden brown, crispy, and cooked through, about 3 minutes. Retrieve with a metal slotted spoon and drain on a paper towel–padded plate.

Sheet-Pan Primer

"Holy Sheet!" is not only the name of the prettiest sheet pan in the land (made by the folks at Great Jones) but also what we exclaimed when we realized cooking on one makes supper a snap, offering the ability to pop dinner in the oven and leave it largely unattended while you join in fireside cocktails. The term "sheet-pan dinner" has generally come to signify an interdisciplinary approach that mixes proteins and produce on the same pan. Once you've tried these recipes as written, we hope you'll have the confidence to play roasting roulette with any number of protein and vegetable combinations, keeping in mind the following tips.

Gray's Anatomy

The sheet-pan technique is particularly suited for cabin life since vacation homes are often stocked with poor-quality pots and skillets but generally have a rimmed 18-by-13-inch (46 by 33 cm) half sheet pan and (if you're lucky) a 9-by-13-inch (23 by 33 cm) quarter sheet pan in the cabinet. (Although given the ease of mind it provides, it can't hurt to pack one in if you're driving to your destination.)

Roast with the Most

Tossing the produce with a healthy glug of olive oil entices the ingredients to roast without burning. Lining the sheet pan with parchment paper hastens cleanup but lessens caramelization. Pick your priority.

Take Space

Use two sheet pans when doubling the recipes, or when you've bought supersize vegetables and the goods are piling up; making contact with the pan is key.

Feel the Heat

Oven temperatures (as a repairperson once told us, to our jaws-dropped surprise) can swing 25 degrees (Fahrenheit—roughly 4 degrees Celsius) and still be considered true, so, especially when working with an unfamiliar oven, use your senses, and give the dish a few more minutes if needed. (If you don't like guesswork, pop your oven thermometer in your bag . . . and hope it's accurate.) Turn vegetables with a spatula midway through the cooking time.

Be Direct

If the vegetables are tender but the protein is still pale (particularly when you're looking to crisp sausages or chicken skin), pop the sheet pan under the broiler for a minute or two until it's brilliantly browned.

Hold for Applause

Transfer it all to a platter . . . or don't! Finish with fresh herbs for maximum oohs and aahs.

Sausages with Roasted Grapes, Shallots, and Sweet Potato Spears

SERVES 4

Any fresh sausage will do for this satisfying sheet-pan supper, be it a bright chorizo, mild Italian, or indulgent Käsekrainer. Nestle the sausages directly on the sheet pan, rather than on top of the grapes, to avoid adorning your links with potentially alarming purple polka dots.

1½ teaspoons ground coriander

1½ teaspoons ground cumin

1½ teaspoons brown sugar

1½ teaspoons kosher salt

1½ teaspoons freshly ground black pepper

¼ teaspoon cayenne pepper

4 sweet potatoes (2 pounds/910 g), peeled and quartered lengthwise

4 shallots, peeled and cut into 6 wedges

1 pound (455 g) seedless red grapes

3 tablespoons extra-virgin olive oil

1½ pounds (680 g) sausages (6 links)

1 tablespoon chopped fresh mint

4 tablespoons (60 ml) red wine vinegar, plus more for drizzling

1. Position a rack in the upper third of the oven and another in the center, and preheat the oven to 425°F (220°C).

2. Mix the coriander, cumin, brown sugar, salt, black pepper, and cayenne in a small bowl. Combine the sweet potatoes, shallots, and grapes in a large bowl. Drizzle with the olive oil, add the spice mixture, and toss to coat.

3. Distribute the sausages evenly on two sheet pans and poke them all over with a fork. Arrange the vegetables and grapes in an even layer around the sausages.

4. Roast for 30 to 35 minutes, turning the sausage, tossing the grapes and vegetables, and rotating the sheet pans once. When the sweet potatoes are tender, switch the oven to broil on high and broil for 1 to 2 minutes to brown the sausages.

5. Transfer the sausages and vegetables and grapes to a platter and sprinkle with the mint. Add 2 tablespoons vinegar to each sheet pan and scrape with a spatula to loosen any browned bits, then drizzle vinegar over the platter. Serve immediately.

Buttermilk Chicken with Roasted Lemons, Torn Sourdough, and Calabrian Chile Sauce

SERVES 4

Thanks to two quick make-ahead kitchen projects (a spicy preserved lemon–spiked sauce and the world's easiest marinade), this winner winner chicken (sheet-pan) dinner packs big flavors with very little active time. If you're not a fan of spicy foods, substitute sun-dried tomatoes for the chiles in the sauce. Serve with braised greens (see page 80) or a green salad.

8 bone-in, skin-on
chicken thighs
2 garlic cloves, crushed
and peeled
1½ cups (360 ml)
buttermilk
Kosher salt
1 teaspoon finely
chopped fresh
oregano

**CALABRIAN CHILE
SAUCE**

2 or 3 Calabrian chiles,
stemmed and seeded
1 preserved lemon, peel
only (rinse, discard
seeds and pulp;
see Tiny Tip)
⅓ cup (80 ml) safflower
oil or other neutral oil
2 teaspoons Dijon
mustard
1 teaspoon dry mustard
1 garlic clove, peeled

1 red bell pepper, thinly
sliced
¼ cup plus 1 teaspoon
(65 ml) extra-virgin
olive oil
2 lemons, halved
1 small loaf sourdough
bread
Kosher salt
4 sprigs oregano,
for garnish

1. Place the chicken thighs and garlic in a large bag or (11-cup/2.6 L or so) lidded storage container. Stir together the buttermilk, 1 tablespoon salt, and the oregano in a large spouted measuring cup and pour the mixture over the chicken. Refrigerate for at least 1 hour and up to 2 days, turning the chicken periodically.

2. Meanwhile, to make the sauce: Combine the chiles, preserved lemon peel, safflower oil, Dijon, dry mustard, garlic, and ¼ cup (60 ml) water in a high-speed blender or food processor and process until smooth. Transfer to a resealable container and refrigerate until ready to use (it will keep for up to 2 weeks).

3. Position a rack in the center of the oven and preheat the oven to 425°F (220°C).

4. Use tongs to transfer the chicken to a rimmed sheet pan, allowing any excess buttermilk to drip back into the bag or container. Mix the bell pepper with 1 teaspoon of the olive oil in a small bowl. Arrange the peppers and lemons around the chicken.

5. Tear the bread into chunks and spread them on a separate sheet pan. Drizzle with the remaining ¼ cup (60 ml) olive oil and mix with your hands, making certain the bread soaks up as much oil as possible. Season with salt.

6. Bake the chicken for 15 minutes, then add the pan with the bread to the oven and bake for 25 to 30 minutes, tossing the bread and rotating both sheet

AT THE CABIN
- **Lidded storage container, for marinating the chicken**
- **High-speed blender or food processor**

pans once, until the chicken is golden brown and the bread is starting to crisp. Remove both sheet pans from the oven and let the chicken rest for 5 minutes.

7. Arrange a bed of torn sourdough in four shallow bowls and top each with two chicken thighs. Divide the peppers evenly among them and pour the pan juices on top. Garnish each bowl with a sprig of oregano and a lemon half. Serve with chile sauce alongside.

TINY TIP: *Look for preserved lemons in major grocery stores or Middle Eastern markets, or make them yourself at home—all you need are lemons, salt, time, and perhaps an internet tutorial. We like Paula Wolfert's method, which is widely available online. To prepare the preserved lemon in this recipe, slice it in half, remove the seeds and pulp, rinse the rind briefly in water, and chop.*

Slow-Roasted Salmon Bowl with Burst Tomatoes and Broccolini

SERVES 4

Shop ahead for this supper for those days that go awry, leaving less time to make dinner than anticipated. Miso keeps for up to a year in the refrigerator, frozen salmon (placed in a resealable bag and submerged in cold water) thaws in an hour, and short-grain brown rice never fails as an ol' reliable. With the main ingredients settled, go forth with the recipe as written or riff with the vegetables you have on hand, swapping in thin asparagus spears, green beans, or red bell peppers for the Broccolini, or adding steamed sweet potato cubes, sautéed baby bok choy, or braised greens to the bowl.

4 (6-ounce/170 g, 1½-inch-thick/4 cm) skin-on salmon fillets
Kosher salt and freshly ground black pepper
4 tablespoons (60 ml) extra-virgin olive oil
¼ cup (60 ml) white wine
2 tablespoons white miso paste
2 tablespoons honey
1 tablespoon fresh lemon juice
2 teaspoons grated fresh ginger
1 garlic clove, minced
1 bunch scallions
2 teaspoons sesame seeds
2 bunches Broccolini (about 2 pounds/910 g), ends trimmed
1 pint (220 g) cherry tomatoes, halved
3 cups (590 g) cooked brown rice
4 soft-boiled eggs, peeled and halved (optional; see Tiny Tips)

1. Position a rack in the center of the oven and a second rack in the top position. Preheat the oven to 300°F (150°C).

2. Set the salmon fillets skin-side down in a shallow dish and season with salt and pepper. Whisk together 2 tablespoons of the olive oil, the wine, miso, honey, lemon juice, ginger, and garlic in a small bowl. Pour all but about 2 tablespoons of the marinade over the salmon (reserve the remainder in the bowl). Marinate on the countertop for 30 minutes.

3. Slice the scallions very thinly on an angle and soak in a bowl of ice water for 30 minutes. Drain and pat dry with paper towels. Add the scallions and sesame seeds to the bowl with the reserved marinade and toss to combine.

4. Toss the Broccolini and tomatoes on a sheet pan with the remaining 2 tablespoons olive oil. Arrange in a single layer. Bake for 10 minutes, then use tongs to remove the salmon from the marinade and nestle it directly on the sheet pan among the vegetables (discard the marinade). Bake for 20 to 25 minutes more, until the salmon is prettily pink and just cooked through, the tomatoes have caramelized, and the Broccolini is tender.

5. Flake the salmon with a fork and discard the skin, or serve the pieces whole. Divide the rice among four bowls and top evenly with the salmon, Broccolini, tomatoes, scallion salad, and, if you wish, a jammy egg. Serve.

TINY TIPS: *To avoid unsightly albumin (that's the official name for the white stuff that can seep from salmon), cook your sheet-pan salmon low and slow and ask at the fish counter for pieces of salmon that are of similar thickness. (Avoid a thinner, tail-end piece, which is apt to overcook.)*

For perfect soft-boiled eggs, bring the eggs to room temperature before cooking. (Twenty minutes on the countertop should do it.) Boil for 6½ minutes, then chill in ice water for 2 minutes before peeling. Slice in half just before serving.

Spaghetti and Meatballs for the Masses

MAKES ABOUT 30 MEATBALLS; PASTA AND SAUCE SERVE 4

Baking your meatballs on a sheet pan rather than cooking them in a skillet allows you to easily scale up—as well as clean up!—supper for a crowd. To keep the meatballs consistently spherical, be certain to preheat the oven, chill the meat until the moment you mix it, and work quickly.

MEATBALLS

2 cups (90 g) fresh bread crumbs
½ cup (120 ml) milk
1 pound (455 g) ground beef
1 pound (455 g) ground pork
1 small onion, finely diced
1 large egg, scrambled
½ cup (50 g) freshly grated Parmesan, plus more for serving
¼ cup (13 g) finely chopped flat-leaf parsley
4 garlic cloves, grated on a Microplane
1 teaspoon grated lemon zest
1 tablespoon kosher salt
1 teaspoon freshly ground black pepper

RED SAUCE

¼ cup (60 ml) extra-virgin olive oil
2 tablespoons tomato paste
2 garlic cloves, minced
1 (28-ounce/795 g) can puréed San Marzano tomatoes
½ teaspoon kosher salt
¼ teaspoon freshly ground black pepper

12 ounces (340 g) dried spaghetti

1. To make the meatballs: Preheat the oven to 425°F (220°C). Line two sheet pans with parchment paper.

2. Combine the bread crumbs and milk in a large bowl and let stand for 2 minutes, until the milk has been completely absorbed. Add the beef, pork, onion, egg, Parmesan, parsley, garlic, lemon zest, salt, and pepper. Gently mix to combine all the ingredients. Roll the meat mixture into walnut-size balls and place them on the prepared sheet pans. Bake for 20 minutes, or until browned and cooked through.

3. Meanwhile, to make the sauce: Heat the olive oil in a large sauté pan or skillet over medium heat. Stir in the tomato paste and cook for 3 minutes, until it turns a darker shade, then add the garlic and cook for 1 minute, until fragrant. Stir in the puréed tomatoes, salt, and pepper. Bring to a boil, then reduce the heat to maintain a simmer and cook for 20 minutes or so as the meatballs bake. Transfer the cooked meatballs to the sauce and simmer on low until ready to serve.

4. Bring a large pot of generously salted water to a boil. Add the spaghetti and cook according to the package instructions. Reserve a ladleful of the pasta water, then drain the spaghetti.

5. Combine the spaghetti, meatballs, sauce, and a splash of the pasta water either in the pan with the sauce (if it's very large) or in the pasta pot, using tongs to move and mix the pasta. Serve topped with grated Parmesan. Store any leftover meatballs as instructed opposite.

Meatball Maestro

If you're not using this entire recipe to feed the masses immediately, you can orchestrate many dinners with your mess of meatballs. They will keep in the refrigerator for up to 4 days and in the freezer for up to 3 months. To freeze nice round individual meatballs (rather than an impenetrable misshapen meatloaf), follow the order of operations and freeze the meatballs *before* bagging. Cool the sheet pan on the countertop, place it in the freezer for an hour, then transfer the meatballs to freezer bags. Defrost before using, then have a ball (sorry, had to) reimagining your meaty marvels. The possibilities start here.

Stromboli: Quarter the meatballs and substitute for the cured meats in the stromboli recipe on page 58.

Sheet-pan pizza: Stretch pizza dough over a sheet pan. Top with sauce, halved meatballs, and dollops of ricotta. Bake in a preheated 450°F (230°C) oven for 20 minutes. Top with fresh basil.

Sub: Simmer the meatballs and red sauce in a skillet over low heat until warmed through. Split hoagie rolls, spread with sauce, and top with meatballs and mozzarella. Set on a sheet pan and broil for 3 to 5 minutes, until the cheese bubbles.

Polenta: Serve meatballs swimming in sauce in a shallow bowl of cheesy polenta, with a glass of Chianti.

Baked ziti skillet: Combine cooked pasta, red sauce, ⅓ cup (50 g) torn green olives, and meatballs in a cast-iron skillet, top with torn mozzarella, and bake in a preheated 325°F (160°C) oven for 30 minutes, or until bubbling.

Grilled bread: Serve meatballs swimming in sauce with thick slices of bread rubbed with garlic, brushed with olive oil, and cooked in a grill pan over high heat until marks form.

Panini: Halve the meatballs and arrange on ciabatta with fork-tender broccoli rabe, provolone, and Calabrian chile peppers. Use a panini press to toast the sandwich and melt the cheese.

Salad: Serve in sauce as a sidecar to an antipasto salad.

Slow cooker: When serving supper in phases—because there are those who night-ski and those who do not—keep meatballs and sauce warm in a slow cooker set to low. Bring a large pot of water to a boil, cover, and turn off the heat. As friends appear, return the water to a boil and cook pasta to order, removing it with tongs to keep the pasta water at the ready.

Italian wedding soup: Add 1 pound (455 g) coarsely chopped escarole, the meatballs, and 1 cup (105 g) small pasta (such as ditalini) to 8 cups (2 L) of simmering stock. Simmer for 10 minutes, until the escarole is tender, the pasta is cooked, and the meatballs are warmed through. Scramble 2 eggs and ¼ cup (25 g) Parmigiano Reggiano in a small bowl and slowly stir into the soup. Serve with additional cheese and freshly ground black pepper.

Ski House Steak with Herb Butter

SERVES 2

Reverse-searing may sound ambitious, but it's really just a nice way to say you can avoid overcooking your grass-fed prize by starting slow, with the steak in the oven, then confidently achieve that perfect crust with a good sear in a piping-hot cast-iron skillet. This method is wonderfully reliable as long as you have a meat thermometer, so be sure to throw one in the duffel. Serve the steak with a Bunny Hill Blue Cheese Wedge (page 77) and a baked potato.

1 (2-inch-thick/5 cm) boneless rib-eye steak
Kosher salt and freshly ground black pepper

HERB BUTTER

½ cup (1 stick/115 g) unsalted butter, at room temperature
2 tablespoons finely chopped fresh flat-leaf parsley
1 teaspoon finely chopped fresh thyme
1 teaspoon finely chopped fresh rosemary
1 teaspoon grated lemon zest
½ teaspoon freshly ground black pepper
½ teaspoon kosher salt

1 tablespoon grapeseed or safflower oil
Watercress, for serving

AT THE CABIN
• Meat thermometer

1. Place the steak on a wire rack on top of a sheet pan. Generously season the steak with salt and pepper and refrigerate for at least 30 minutes.

2. To make the herb butter: Use a fork (with a smooshing motion) or a food processor to combine the butter, parsley, thyme, rosemary, lemon zest, pepper, and salt. Transfer the compound butter to a widemouthed 8-ounce (240 ml) mason jar and refrigerate until ready to use (it will keep for up to 2 weeks).

3. Preheat the oven to 225°F (110°C).

4. Transfer the pan with the steak to the oven and cook until the internal temperature reaches 105°F (40°C) for rare, 115°F (46°C) for medium-rare, 125°F (52°C) for medium, or 135°F (57°C) for medium-well, about 30 minutes for medium.

5. Heat a 12-inch (30 cm) cast-iron skillet over high heat for 6 to 10 minutes, until smoking. Add the grapeseed or safflower oil and use tongs to rotate the steak to sear all the edges. Lay the steak flat and cook until the steak is well browned and easily comes away from the skillet, 45 seconds to 1 minute on each side.

6. Transfer the steak to a wooden cutting board and let rest for 2 minutes. Slice on an angle into ½-inch-thick (1.2 cm) pieces. Add a few pats of herb butter on top and serve the steak on the board to share.

Food First-Aid Kit

Load up a first-aid storage box so you'll be ready for emergencies of every variety, even if it's just a cocoa craving.

1. Knitting needles **2.** Swiss Mister cocoa mix or Drinking Chocolate (page 186) **3.** Maple syrup **4.** Whiskey **5.** Instant espresso **6.** Pure vanilla extract **7.** Cinnamon sticks **8.** Gingerbread spice (see Tiny Tips, page 165) **9.** Honey **10.** Salt and pepper **11.** Matches **12.** Assorted tea **13.** Band-Aids—may you never need them.

Wanna Sauna?
A Manners Manifesto

If it's been a while, or never, since you've parked yourself on a bench inside a sweltering cedar box, clad only in your birthday suit, with a group of complete strangers, you may need a few reminders on proper sauna sweat-iquette before embarking on your Lake Hornavan holiday.

Naked Truth

Quite often, saunas are no-clothes zones, so be prepared to bare your buns (just remember, nobody's looking at you) (okay, maybe they are, but you'll never see these people again) (unless it turns out they're staying in the ice hut next door). However, depending on the sauna situation—some are coed—a cover-up may be called for, be that a towel or a swimsuit. Double-check the apparel policy before you go, or pack a suit just in case.

Shower Power

Since saunas are all about banishing toxins, it stands to reason that everyone within should be as pristine as possible to begin with, so shower before you step inside. In that same sanitary vein, spread your towel over the sauna bench before sitting/lying down/doing hot yoga on it.

Personal Space Race

Many saunas run on the compact side, so respect the personal space and serenity of your fellow perspirers. Stepping on other people as you climb to the top tier, randomly braiding the hair of the person on the bench below you, and any sort of audible bodily function are all no-nos (if your stomach's growling, go have a handful of Moose Chow, page 41).

Door Dash

This one pretty much goes without saying, but unless you want to hear a rousing chorus of "Oletko syntynyt navetassa?!?" (Were you born in a barn?!?) upon entering/exiting the sauna, make it quick, to minimize goose-bump-inducing gusts of cold air.

Pour One Out

The bucket of water and ladle near the sauna coals are the two ingredients you need to cook up a cleansing cloud of *löyly*, the Finnish word for sauna steam. To skirt both steam burns and lectures from stern-looking Scandinavians, start with one or two scoops; drizzle, don't dump; and always use the ladle.

Talk Is Deep

Some saunas are silent, especially in the United States, and some are social (see: Finland); go with the flow depending on the setting. While you may want to sidestep heavy conversation hitters like politics, religion, and exactly which carrying technique will ensure victory in the annual Wife Carrying World Championships (yes, it's a real thing), safe topics include travel, movies, the funniest gaffes you saw that day on the slopes, and favorite après-ski recipes (see: Cranberry-Cardamom Glogg, page 175).

Onsen Zen

Should your winter wonderland be in the shadow of Mount Yōtei, when it comes to recreational overheating, you'll be dripping *and* dipping—into one of Japan's thousands of onsen, or hot springs. While the scenery is quite different, several of the preceding principles apply, especially the birthday suit (mandatory) and showering (meticulously and communally) bits. Talking is acceptable; tattoos are still often not (sorry, Ben Affleck; this is not the time for your giant Technicolor back phoenix to rise).

Brrrisket with Parsley and Pomegranate

SERVES 6 TO 8

Bright pops of color, thanks to pomegranate arils and parsley, make this homey classic a head-turner once more. Brisket is easiest to slice after it's been chilled, so make it ahead—up to 5 days, even—store it in the fridge, and follow the instructions in step 4 to warm it before serving. If you don't have a slow cooker on hand, you could also braise the brisket in a Dutch oven for 4 to 5 hours at 325°F (160°C) one evening, and warm it up the next. Serve with egg noodles tossed in butter, mashed potatoes, or Parsnip Mash.

1 flat-cut beef brisket (about 5 pounds/ 2.3 kg)

Kosher salt and freshly ground black pepper

4 tablespoons (60 ml) grapeseed, safflower, or canola oil

2 celery stalks, chopped

1 large yellow onion, thinly sliced

1 fennel bulb, thinly sliced

2 tablespoons tomato paste

6 garlic cloves, smashed

2 cups (480 ml) stock (chicken, beef, or vegetable)

1 (14.5-ounce/411 g) can diced tomatoes with their juices

1 teaspoon paprika

2 bay leaves

3 allspice berries

½ cup (90 g) pomegranate arils

¼ cup (13 g) chopped fresh flat-leaf parsley

2 teaspoons red wine vinegar

Cooked egg noodles, mashed potatoes, or Parsnip Mash (see Tiny Tip), for serving

1. Generously season the brisket with salt and pepper. Heat 2 tablespoons of the grapeseed oil in a large cast-iron skillet over medium-high heat. Sear the brisket, using tongs to turn it over after about 10 minutes, until well browned on both sides. Remove from the heat and transfer the brisket to a plate. Set aside.

2. Pour off the oil and return the skillet to the stovetop. Heat the remaining 2 tablespoons oil over medium heat. Add the celery, onion, and fennel and cook, stirring frequently, for 8 minutes, until the vegetables are softened and the onions are translucent. Add the tomato paste and garlic and cook, stirring to coat the vegetables in the paste, for 2 minutes. Remove from the heat.

3. Stir together the stock, diced tomatoes and their juices, and paprika in a slow cooker. Add the cooked vegetables. Nestle in the brisket and add the bay leaves and allspice. Cover and cook on low for 8 hours, until the meat is very tender when pierced with a knife. (At this point, the brisket may be cooled on the countertop, transferred to an airtight container, and refrigerated for up to 5 days before serving.)

4. To serve, transfer the brisket to a wooden cutting board and slice it against the grain. Skim the fat from the gravy. If desired, blend the gravy a bit using an immersion blender or strain it through a fine-mesh strainer (not required—we often do neither!). Return the

- **Slow cooker**

sliced brisket and gravy to the slow cooker or transfer them to a skillet over low heat, and gently simmer until the meat is warmed through, about 10 minutes.

5. Mix the pomegranate arils, parsley, and vinegar in a small bowl. Arrange the brisket slices on a platter of egg noodles, mashed potatoes, or Parsnip Mash, ladle gravy on top, garnish with the pomegranate and parsley topping, and serve immediately.

TINY TIP: *If you've maxed out on mashed potatoes, make a creamy Parsnip Mash: Boil 2 pounds (910 g) parsnips (peeled, halved lengthwise, then cut crosswise into 2-inch/5 cm chunks) in a large pot of salted water until tender, 15 to 20 minutes. Meanwhile, combine 1 cup (240 ml) cream, 1 cup (240 ml) milk, and 6 smashed and peeled garlic cloves in a saucepan over medium heat. Bring to a boil, then reduce the heat and simmer for 15 minutes. Place the parsnips in a blender and strain the garlic-infused cream on top. Add 4 tablespoons (½ stick/60 g) unsalted butter, 1½ teaspoons kosher salt, and ½ teaspoon freshly ground black pepper and blend until smooth. Smooth over a platter and arrange the sliced brisket on top. Makes 4 cups (1 L).*

Brandy-Braised Short Ribs with Carrots

SERVES 4

Braise to amaze. The beauty of this technique is that all the effort is up front, so you can make the dish ahead to reheat later, and instead of spending the afternoon cooking, spend it perfecting your figure eight, tobogganing with your little loons, or driving to the cabin and revealing, to everyone's relief, that dinner is already in the bag. (Thanks to your Dutch oven carrier.) When meat is the main event, make friends with the butcher to get the pick of the case. Ask for eight of the choicest short ribs, around 2 inches (5 cm) thick. This recipe makes plenty of sauce, all the better to spoon over popovers (see page 86), spaetzle, polenta, or mashed potatoes.

2 tablespoons grapeseed oil
8 bone-in beef short ribs (see Tiny Tips)
Kosher salt and freshly ground black pepper
9 medium carrots: 3 chopped, 6 halved lengthwise
2 celery stalks, chopped
1 large onion, chopped
6 garlic cloves, smashed and peeled
2 tablespoons tomato paste
2 cups (480 ml) dry red wine
½ cup (120 ml) brandy
1 sprig rosemary
6 sprigs thyme
8 cups (2 L) beef stock
8 cipollini onions, halved
¼ cup (13 g) minced fresh parsley
1 tablespoon prepared horseradish
2 teaspoons grated lemon zest
Spaetzle (see page 89), mashed potatoes, or other starch, for serving

1. Position a rack in the center of the oven and preheat the oven to 325°F (160°C).

2. Heat the grapeseed oil in a large Dutch oven over high heat. Generously season the short ribs with salt and pepper. Working in batches, sear the short ribs, using tongs to turn them after about 3 minutes, until well browned on each side. (If the short ribs stick to the pot when you try to turn them, let them sear for another minute. The pot will let go when it's ready, much like you when you're finally hauling the Christmas tree to the curb in February.) Transfer the ribs to a plate and tie with kitchen twine (see Tiny Tips).

3. Pour off all but 2 tablespoons of the fat from the Dutch oven. Reduce the heat to medium and add the chopped carrots, celery, onion, and garlic to the pot. Cook, stirring frequently, for 8 minutes, until the vegetables are softened and the onions are translucent. Stir in the tomato paste and cook, stirring to coat the vegetables, for 2 minutes more.

4. Add the wine and brandy and cook, scraping up any browned bits from the bottom of the pot with a wooden spoon, for 3 minutes. Return the short ribs to the pot, add the rosemary and thyme, and pour in the stock; it should cover the short ribs by 1 inch (2.5 cm). (In a 9-quart/9 L Dutch oven, that takes all 2 quarts/2 L.

If you're short on stock, add water.) Cover the pot and transfer it to the oven. Braise until the meat is fork-tender, 3 to 3½ hours.

5. Transfer the short ribs to an airtight container. Strain the sauce through a fine-mesh sieve and discard the solids, including all the spent vegetables and herbs. Return the sauce to the pot and cover. Refrigerate the short ribs and sauce overnight. (Refrigerating the sauce in a separate container makes for easiest next-day skimming.)

6. Discard the fat that has hardened on the top of the sauce. Set the pot over high heat and bring the sauce to a boil, then turn the heat to medium and simmer for 30 minutes to reduce the sauce. Add the split carrots, the cipollini onions, and the short ribs, cover, and simmer for 15 minutes more, until the short ribs are warmed through and the carrots are fork-tender.

7. Mix together the parsley, horseradish, and lemon zest with a fork in a small bowl (see Tiny Tips). Transfer the short ribs to a platter of spaetzle, mashed potatoes, or any starchy side that suits your fancy, and sprinkle the short ribs with the horseradish gremolata. Serve immediately.

TINY TIPS: *For the most becoming presentation, tie a piece of kitchen twine around each rib after searing to keep the meat from falling off the bone during the braise. (Remove before serving.) The horseradish gremolata topping is also delicious stirred into polenta, egg noodles, or mashed potatoes. If you're planning for it to do double duty as such, double the recipe and mix half into the aforementioned starch.*

Chalet Cassoulet

SERVES 4

You may not have the time/patience/dedicated refrigerator space to properly prepare a three-day cassoulet at your cabin; nevertheless, the comforting combination of beans, meats, and bread crumbs is well within reach via this one-dish riff, which fits best in a 5-quart (5 L) enamelware braiser or 12-inch (30 cm) skillet, travels beautifully from oven to table, and needs no accompaniments.

4 bone-in, skin-on chicken thighs
Kosher salt and freshly ground black pepper
2 tablespoons grapeseed oil
3 cups (540 g) cooked white beans (such as Tarbais, cannellini, or great northern; see Tiny Tips)
1 cup (240 ml) chicken stock
1 large onion, chopped
1 medium carrot, chopped
6 ounces (170 g) smoked sausage, such as kielbasa, cut on an angle into ½-inch-thick (1.2 cm) coins
4 garlic cloves, chopped
1 tablespoon tomato paste
1 tablespoon fresh thyme leaves
1 bay leaf
2 thick slices country bread
1 tablespoon olive oil
1 tablespoon finely chopped fresh parsley, for garnish

AT THE CABIN
• Braiser

1. Position a rack in the center of the oven and preheat the oven to 375°F (190°C).

2. Season the chicken with salt and pepper. Warm the grapeseed oil in a 5-quart (5 L) braiser or 12-inch (30 cm) cast-iron skillet over medium-high heat. Add the chicken to the pot, skin-side down, and cook until well browned and crisp on the first side, about 10 minutes. Turn the chicken and cook until browned on the second side, about 8 minutes more. Use tongs to move the chicken to a plate, leaving the rendered fat in the skillet.

3. Meanwhile, combine 1 cup (180 g) of the beans and the stock in a blender or food processor and blend until smooth. Set aside.

4. Return the braiser or skillet to medium heat. Add the onion and carrot and cook, stirring frequently, until soft, 8 minutes. Use a wooden spoon to push the vegetables to the side of the pan, then add the kielbasa and cook for a few minutes, until the edges begin to brown and crisp. Stir together the sausage and vegetables. Add the garlic, tomato paste, thyme, and bay leaf and stir to coat. Add the puréed bean mixture and the remaining 2 cups (360 g) whole beans and bring to a simmer, stirring and scraping the bottom of the pan to release any browned bits. Season with ½ teaspoon pepper and a little salt if you think it needs it (kielbasa can be plenty salty). Use tongs to nestle the chicken thighs on top of the beans, then transfer the pot to the oven. Bake for 30 minutes, until a skin has formed on top of the beans.

5. Meanwhile, pulse the sliced bread in a food processor to break it into rustic (not too fine) crumbs. Warm the olive oil in a skillet over medium heat. Stir in the bread crumbs, add a pinch of salt, and cook, tossing often to coat, for 5 minutes, until crisp and toasty brown. Remove from the heat.

6. Remove the pot from the oven and discard the bay leaf. Sprinkle the bread crumbs on top of the cassoulet, garnish with the parsley, and serve directly from the pot.

TINY TIPS: *If you have any heirloom beans tucked in the pantry, this is their moment to shine.*

Protect the table from searing-hot cast iron with a trivet. If it's too late, and you are now staring, aghast, at white heat stains on laminated wood in a rental cabin, try this before you lose hope (and/or your deposit): Mix toothpaste and baking soda to make a paste. Rub the paste into the stain. Wipe with a damp cloth; the stain should lift. Buff with furniture polish or mineral oil.

CHAPTER 5

Desserts

No need for your sweet tooth to hibernate with the bears, bats, and bees—there's still so much sugary good fun to be had with the fall and winter seasons' natural bounty: elegant long-necked pears primed for Burnt Honey and Thyme Roasted Pears, rosy-cheeked apples just waiting to be tucked into a Calvados Cake or stuffed into flaky sweet-tart Apple-Cranberry Strudel, bright and vibrant citrus perfect for building a showstopping Almond-Tangerine Trifle, and, of course, good old bananas, which are always there for you, in times of snow, rain, heat, and gloom of night, just like the postal service but far better suited for baking into a Banana Tarte Tatin with Dark Rum Sauce.

Six Sweets Made with Snow

There's no shortage of winter's most evocative ingredient: fresh *clean* snow.

1. Snow Cone

Pack freshly fallen snow in a paper cone, drizzle with kumquat syrup (see Tiny Tips, page 165), and enjoy.

2. Snowfoggato

Pack a tight snowball and place in a clear mug. Stir a spoonful of sugar into a shot of espresso and pour over the snowball. Pour in 2 ounces (60 ml) sambuca, and top with whipped cream and shaved chocolate. Cin cin!

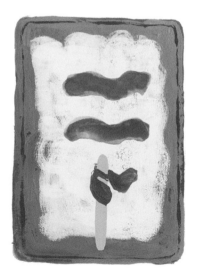

3. Sugar on Snow

Channel your inner Laura Ingalls Wilder and bring pans of freshly fallen snow into your little house, whether or not it's in the Big Woods. Heat maple syrup to 235°F (113°C), drizzle patterns over the snow, and twirl the maple taffy onto an ice pop stick.

4. Snow Ice Cream

Whisk ¾ cup (180 ml) heavy cream, 1 teaspoon pure vanilla extract, and ½ cup (65 g) confectioners' sugar together in a metal bowl until combined. Add 6 cups (1.5 L) freshly fallen snow, stir until thickened, scoop, and serve. Cherry on top optional.

5. Frozen Hot Chocolate

Make 1 cup (240 ml) Swiss Mister (page 186) or Drinking Chocolate (page 186) and let cool. Pour the cooled hot chocolate over 6 cups (1.5 L) freshly fallen snow and stir until soft. Scoop into two bowls and top with whipped cream and chocolate sprinkles.

6. Piña Snowlada

Boil 1½ cups (360 ml) pineapple juice in a saucepan over high heat until reduced to ¼ cup (60 ml). Stir 1 cup (240 ml) coconut milk into 6 cups (1.5 L) freshly fallen snow. Scoop into two bowls, top each with 2 ounces (60 ml) dark rum, a drizzle of the pineapple syrup, a sprinkle of coconut flakes, and a paper umbrella.

Off-Piste Orangettes

MAKES 72 TO 96 CHOCOLATE-COATED ORANGE PEELS

Don't let the deliciously fragrant orange peels generated by making Winter Citrus Salad (page 195) go to waste—candy them! We forgo the traditional sugar toss in favor of a simple and less-sugary chocolate dip, but if you're craving the classic candied version with a sweet crunch, once the peels have finished their simmer, combine a handful of peels with a handful of sugar in a resealable bag or container and shake until fully coated; then remove, add another handful of peels (and sugar as needed) and repeat, until all the peels are dusted with sugar.

3 thick-skinned oranges
3 cups (600 g) sugar
3 ounces (85 g) bittersweet chocolate, chopped or chips (about ½ cup)

1. Line a rimmed half sheet pan with parchment paper and place a wire rack on top. Fill a large saucepan halfway with water and bring the water to a boil over high heat.

2. While the water is heating, trim ¼ inch (6 mm) off the top and bottom of each orange. Cutting from top to bottom, score the orange skin on all four sides, then peel off the skin (pith, too) in four sections. Reserve the fruit for juicing, eating as a snack, or a citrus salad.

3. Slice each section of peel lengthwise into ¼-inch-wide (6 mm) strips (you should get 6 to 8 strips per section). Boil the peels for 5 minutes, stirring often, then drain in a colander. Return the peels to the saucepan, refill it with cold water, swish the peels around to rinse, then drain them again. Refill the pot, bring the water to a boil, and boil the peels for 5 minutes more, then drain, refill the pot, rinse, and drain again; this helps banish any bitterness (the oranges', at least—you're on your own).

4. Combine the sugar and 3 cups (720 ml) water in the saucepan. Bring to a boil over medium-high heat, stirring to dissolve the sugar, then reduce the heat to maintain an enthusiastic simmer. Add the peels and simmer, stirring often, until soft and slightly translucent but not falling apart, 45 minutes to 1 hour. Keep an eye on them to ensure that the syrup doesn't get too hot and bubble over or burn.

5. Drain the peels, reserving the syrup for another use (see Tiny Tips). Spread the peels out on the wire rack with tongs. Let dry until no longer tacky to the touch (at least 1 day and up to 2 days; plan accordingly).

6. When the peels are dry, place the chocolate in a small heatproof bowl and set the bowl over a saucepan of simmering water (be sure the bottom of the bowl doesn't touch the water). Heat, stirring, until the chocolate has melted. Remove the rack of peels from the sheet pan, leaving the parchment behind. Dip each peel about halfway into the chocolate, then transfer to the parchment. When all the peels are dipped, transfer the sheet pan to the refrigerator and let the chocolate set for 15 minutes. Eat the orangettes immediately, pop them into jars and gift to the cabin dwellers next door, or store in an airtight container in the refrigerator for up to 1 month.

TINY TIPS: *If you want to add a little extra zest (literally) to a batch of scones, muffins, or quick bread, forgo the chocolate-dipping step and dice a handful of candied orange peel before tossing it into the dough or batter.*

Spike the leftover orange syrup with a couple tablespoons of Cointreau and store it in a mason jar in the refrigerator for up to 1 month. Use it to sweeten tea, cocktails, mocktails, or homemade orange soda; to moisten pound cake; or just to pour over vanilla bean or dulce de leche ice cream.

Lemon-Pistachio Snowballs

MAKES 24

Also known as Mexican wedding cookies, Russian tea cakes, sandies, butterballs, and can't-eat-just-ones, these delicate lemon-kissed cookies are so tasty that nobody would ever waste one throwing it at your back, which gives them a significant advantage over actual snowballs. If you aren't nuts about pistachios (*what?!*), try almonds, walnuts, pecans, or hazelnuts.

COOKIES

⅓ cup (45 g) shelled roasted pistachios
1 cup (125 g) all-purpose flour
⅛ teaspoon kosher salt
½ cup (1 stick/115 g) unsalted butter, at room temperature
¼ cup (30 g) confectioners' sugar
½ teaspoon pure vanilla extract
1 teaspoon grated lemon zest
2 teaspoons fresh lemon juice (see Tiny Tip)

COATING

⅓ cup (40 g) confectioners' sugar, plus 1 teaspoon for dusting
1 teaspoon grated lemon zest, plus more for garnish

AT THE CABIN

- **Food processor (optional)**
- **Small fine-mesh strainer**
- **Microplane grater**

1. To make the cookies: Preheat the oven to 350°F (180°C). Line a sheet pan with parchment paper.

2. Grind the pistachios in a food processor until finely chopped, 10 to 15 seconds (or coarsely chop by hand if you want the nuts in bigger chunks). Transfer the ground pistachios to a small bowl, add the flour and salt, and mix to combine.

3. Cream the butter, confectioners' sugar, and vanilla in the bowl of a stand mixer fitted with the paddle attachment on medium speed until smooth and creamy, about 1 minute. Mix in the lemon zest and lemon juice. Add the pistachio-flour mixture and beat until the dough comes together.

4. Roll the dough into 24 balls, each about the size of a 1-inch (2.5 cm) jingle bell. Place the balls on the prepared sheet pan, 1½ inches (4 cm) apart. Bake the cookies until the tops are slightly cracked and the bottoms are lightly browned, 12 to 14 minutes. Let the cookies cool on the sheet pan for 10 minutes.

5. To make the coating: Combine the confectioners' sugar and lemon zest in a shallow bowl. Gently roll the cookies in the lemon sugar until coated, then store in an airtight container at room temperature for up to 5 days or in the freezer for up to 1 month. Before serving, use a small fine-mesh strainer to dust them with more confectioners' sugar, and grate fresh lemon zest over the top.

TINY TIP: *For a citrus twist, use orange or lime zest and juice in place of the lemon.*

Variations: For Pink Peppermint Snowballs, omit the lemon and add ½ teaspoon peppermint extract along with the vanilla and crushed candy canes to the coating (pink glitter sprinkles optional). Green tea lovers, make Matcha Meltaways by omitting the lemon and adding 2 teaspoons matcha powder to the dry ingredients.

Huzzah for the Spa

When tired legs get the best of you, treat yourself to this (very) local day spa menu. Most ingredients, including citric acid, can be found in small quantities in the bulk bins.

Borrowed Boots Foot Soak
MAKES 1

¾ cup (195 g) Epsom salts
1 tablespoon carrier oil, such as almond
⅛ teaspoon tea tree essential oil

Fill a basin with 6 quarts (6 L) warm water. Add the Epsom salts, carrier oil, and essential oil. Soak your feet for 20 minutes to assuage any worries about rental-boot germs; tea tree oil has you covered.

Summer Skin Sugar Scrub
MAKES ABOUT 1 CUP (240 ML)

½ cup (100 g) sugar
½ cup (130 g) Himalayan salt or
   Epsom salts
¼ cup (10 g) loose green tea
¾ cup (180 ml) organic coconut oil,
   melted
5 drops lemongrass essential oil

Whisk together the sugar, salt, and green tea in a medium bowl. Add the coconut oil and lemongrass oil. Store the scrub in an airtight container for up to 1 month. To use, gently rub over your skin, rinse with warm water, and teleport to Hawaii.

OPEN 24/7

Bluebird Day Bath Bonbons

MAKES 2

½ cup (90 g) baking soda
¼ cup (30 g) cornstarch
¼ cup (35 g) citric acid
¼ cup (65 g) Epsom salts
2 to 3 tablespoons organic coconut oil,
    melted
2 teaspoons vegetable glycerin
⅛ teaspoon lavender essential oil
5 drops eucalyptus essential oil
10 drops blue soap colorant

In a large bowl, whisk together the
baking soda, cornstarch, citric acid,
and Epsom salts. In a small lidded
container, combine 2 tablespoons
coconut oil, the glycerin, essential oils,
and colorant; shake well. Whisk the
liquid mixture into the dry ingredients,
adding an additional tablespoon of
coconut oil, if necessary, to create the
texture of wet sand. Pack the mixture
into both sides of a 2½-inch (6.35 cm)
spherical mold and press together.
Release from the mold and repeat. Dry
for at least 1 hour, ideally overnight,
before using. Store in an airtight
container. Add one to bathwater for a
soothing, fizzy soak.

Dark Mint Chocolate Cold Snaps

MAKES 24 COOKIES

A handful of rice flour renders these crisp dark chocolate shortbreads irresistibly light and tender, but if you haven't got any in the cabin, all all-purpose it is. Stick to the recipe's melted mint chocolate dip, or try melted raspberry or orange-infused chocolate with a pinch of crumbled freeze-dried raspberries or grated orange zest garnish, respectively.

⅔ cup (80 g) all-purpose flour
¼ cup (40 g) white rice flour
⅓ cup (30 g) unsweetened cocoa powder, sifted
¼ teaspoon kosher salt
½ cup (1 stick/115 g) unsalted butter, at room temperature
¼ cup (50 g) sugar
3 ounces (85 g) mint-flavored dark chocolate, melted
Flaky sea salt or crushed candy canes, for garnish (optional)

1. Whisk together the all-purpose flour, rice flour, cocoa powder, and kosher salt in a small bowl.

2. Cream the butter and sugar in the bowl of a stand mixer fitted with the paddle attachment on medium speed until light and fluffy, about 2 minutes. With the mixer on low speed, slowly add the dry ingredients to the butter mixture, mixing until a soft crumbly dough forms.

3. Transfer the dough to a piece of plastic wrap. Shape it into a 2-inch-diameter (5 cm) log and chill for at least 30 minutes and up to 3 days. (The dough can also be frozen for up to 1 month; let it sit out at room temperature until pliable before slicing.)

4. Preheat the oven to 350°F (180°C). Line a rimmed half sheet pan with parchment paper.

5. Slice the dough into ¼-inch-thick (6 mm) rounds and arrange them on the prepared sheet pan about 1 inch (2.5 cm) apart. Refrigerate for 10 minutes. Bake until the bottoms are dry and the cookies are crisp and snappy, 13 to 15 minutes. Remove from the oven and let cool completely on the pan.

6. Dip each cookie halfway into the melted chocolate, return it to the baking sheet, and sprinkle with a pinch of flaky salt or crushed candy cane. Transfer to the refrigerator and let set for 15 minutes. Store the cookies in an airtight container at room temperature for up to 3 days or in the freezer for up to 1 month.

Caffè Corretto Mousse

SERVES 6

This light and velvety chocolate mousse is an ode to Italy's popular caffè corretto, that dream team of espresso and a splash of something slightly stronger, just the ticket after a long winter's day spent watching Fellini films. Have fun experimenting with different liqueurs (or omit the liqueur), layer in berries or Tangerine Dream Curd (page 153), sprinkle citrus zest or crushed nuts on top, drizzle with caramel or berry sauce, or accessorize with an Amarena cherry, rose petal, lingue di gatto (cat's tongue cookie), and/or tiny Italian flag.

1½ cups (360 ml) heavy cream
6 ounces (170 g) good-quality dark chocolate (60 to 70% cacao), finely chopped, plus more for grating
2 teaspoons instant espresso, such as Medaglia d'Oro
⅛ teaspoon kosher salt
2 tablespoons espresso liqueur, brandy, or dark rum
4 large eggs, separated
1 teaspoon sugar
¼ teaspoon pure vanilla extract

AT THE CABIN
• Microplane grater

1. Stir together ¼ cup (60 ml) of the heavy cream, the chocolate, instant espresso, and salt in a small saucepan over low heat until the chocolate is melted and everything is well blended (the mixture may look grainy; it will turn out fine). Remove from the heat and whisk in 1 tablespoon of the liqueur, then add the egg yolks, one at a time, whisking until smooth. Let cool completely.

2. Whip ¾ cup (180 ml) of the cream in a large bowl until soft peaks form. Whisk half the cooled chocolate mixture into the whipped cream until combined, then whisk in the rest. Beat the egg whites in a separate large bowl with a handheld or stand mixer until soft peaks form. Gently fold the egg whites into the chocolate cream. (If you find raw egg whites as unnerving as a glass-bottom gondola, leave them out; you'll end up with closer to four portions, and the mousse will be denser, but still very delicious.)

3. Divide the mousse among six widemouthed 8-ounce (240 ml) mason jars (or mugs, or wineglasses, or whatever you've got on hand). Cover and chill for at least 4 hours, preferably 8 hours or overnight, and up to 3 days.

4. Just before serving, combine the remaining ½ cup (120 ml) cream, remaining 1 tablespoon liqueur, the sugar, and the vanilla in a large bowl and whip until soft peaks form. Dollop whipped cream on top of each mousse cup and use a Microplane or box grater to shave chocolate over the top, then serve.

Maple Walnut–Whisky Butter Tarts

MAKES 12

Inspired by the many, *many* melt-in-your-mouth butter tarts we've detoured for en route to Whistler, British Columbia, this version of one of our northern neighbor's most hallowed sweets is stuffed with walnuts and spiked with Canadian whisky and pure maple syrup . . . O Canada, indeed! If rye flour is proving as elusive as a hoary marmot sighting (fun fact: the hoary marmot's distinct danger-warning whistle is Whistler's namesake), use whole wheat flour instead.

CRUST

1 cup (125 g) all-purpose flour
½ cup (50 g) rye flour
½ teaspoon kosher salt
10 tablespoons (1¼ sticks/145 g) cold unsalted butter, cut into cubes, plus more for greasing
4 to 6 tablespoons (60 to 90 ml) ice-cold water

FILLING

4 tablespoons (½ stick/ 60 g) unsalted butter, melted
½ cup packed (110 g) dark brown sugar
2 large eggs
⅓ cup (80 ml) pure maple syrup
1 tablespoon all-purpose flour
2 tablespoons Canadian whisky or bourbon
1 teaspoon pure vanilla extract
½ teaspoon kosher salt
1 heaping cup (120 g) chopped walnuts

AT THE CABIN

- Rolling pin (or a Gibson's Finest whisky bottle)

1. To make the crust: Whisk together the all-purpose flour, rye flour, and salt in a large bowl. Add the butter and work it into the flour mixture with your hands (pretend you're snapping your fingers together) until coarse crumbs form. Add the water 2 tablespoons at a time, working it in with your hands until a crumbly dough forms (when you pinch it with your fingers, it should hold together). Press the dough into a 1-inch-thick (2.5 cm) rectangle, wrap it in plastic wrap, and refrigerate for at least 30 minutes and up to 3 days (remove from the refrigerator and let soften for 15 minutes or so before rolling it out).

2. Preheat the oven to 375°F (190°C). Brush a standard 12-cup muffin tin with melted butter.

3. Divide the dough into 12 equal pieces using a pastry scraper or sharp knife. Roll each piece into a ball, then roll out each ball on a lightly floured surface (or between sheets of parchment paper) into a 4-inch (10 cm) round, roughly ⅛ inch (3 mm) thick. Lightly press each round into a prepared muffin cup. Chill the muffin tin in the refrigerator for 10 minutes.

4. Meanwhile, to make the filling: Whisk together the melted butter, brown sugar, eggs, maple syrup, flour, whisky, vanilla, and salt in a medium bowl.

5. Divide the walnuts among the muffin cups, then divide the filling evenly among the cups, pouring it over the walnuts. Bake the tarts until they're golden brown and the filling is set, 25 to 30 minutes. Remove them from the oven, let cool for a few minutes, then gently

remove the tarts from the pan and transfer to a wire rack to continue cooling.

6. Serve the tarts warm, or let cool completely and store in an airtight container in the refrigerator for up to 3 days or in the freezer for up to 1 month; if frozen, wrap in aluminum foil and rewarm in a preheated 350°F (180°C) oven for 15 minutes before serving.

TINY TIPS: *Experiment with add-ins—mix and match currants, raisins, dried cranberries, dried cherries, hazelnuts, pecans, chocolate chunks, shredded coconut, and/or orange zest.*

Should you decide to crown the tarts with scoops of vanilla bean ice cream or dollops of whisky whipped cream (1 cup/240 ml heavy cream + 2 tablespoons light brown sugar + 1 tablespoon whisky), nobody will complain (in true polite Canadian style).

You Need an Altitude Adjustment

Above 3,000 feet (914 m) is generally considered high altitude for cooking purposes, so whether your winter burrow's in Boone, North Carolina (3,333 feet/1,016 m), or Blue River, Colorado (10,036 feet/3,059 m), a few recipe adjustments may be in order thanks to the lower air pressure (although, in many cases, sea-level recipes will turn out just fine at higher altitudes). As a general rule, consider adding an additional tablespoon or two of liquid to account for faster evaporation; help fortify cell structure by slightly reducing fat, sugar, and leavening and/or adding an extra egg and spoonful of flour; decrease proofing times for yeast doughs; and increase baking temperatures by 15° to 25°F (8° to 14°C). Since the specifics of this subject could easily fill a separate book, we suggest you consult Colorado State University's handy High Altitude Food Preparation guide, found on their website (foodsmartcolorado.colostate.edu), for the detailed particulars on everything from canning and candy-making in the clouds to baking perfect sky-high pies and pound cakes.

MENU

DINNER IN THE DOLOMITES

Just what Nonna ordered: a night of meatballs, mangia!, and merriment

One Fine Tinned Fish-nic   53

**Snowdrift Salad with
Anchovy Bread Crumbs**   74

Garlic Rosemary Butter Buns   85

A mess of Meatballs   126

**Braised Greens with
Feta, Preserved Lemon, and Chiles**   80

Caffè Corretto Mousse   149

The house red

Blood Orange Negronis   177

Tangerine Dream Curd

MAKES ABOUT 2 CUPS (480 ML)

This curd takes minutes to make but has long-lasting culinary impact—layer it into an Almond-Tangerine Trifle (page 154), dip warm aebleskiver (see page 196) into it, serve it with shortbread, stir it into yogurt and sprinkle with pistachios, or eat it out of the jar with a spoon.

1 tablespoon grated
tangerine zest
½ cup (120 ml) fresh
tangerine juice
½ cup (100 g) sugar
¼ cup (60 ml) fresh
lemon juice
6 large egg yolks
½ cup (1 stick/115 g)
unsalted butter,
cut into cubes

AT THE CABIN

• **Fine-mesh sieve**

1. Set a fine-mesh sieve over a medium bowl and have a spatula nearby (you'll need them at the end).

2. Whisk together the tangerine zest, tangerine juice, sugar, lemon juice, and egg yolks in a small saucepan over medium heat. Whisk in the butter, a few cubes at a time, and cook, whisking continuously (don't let the mixture boil), until the curd is thick enough to coat the back of a spoon (about the consistency of loose sour cream) and registers 160°F (71°C) on an instant-read thermometer, 5 to 7 minutes.

3. Remove the curd from the heat and pour it slowly through the sieve into the bowl, gently stirring and scraping with the spatula to pass the curd through. (This traps the zest and any lingering lumps, which can be discarded.) Pour the curd into a pint (480 ml) jar, cover, and store in the refrigerator for up to 3 days, although the fresher, the better, flavor-wise.

Almond-Tangerine Trifle

SERVES 8

You may not have a bona fide trifle bowl lying around the cabin, but you likely have a glass bowl or large glass vase; or, finish up that last round of old-fashioneds, then use your whiskey tumblers as individual trifle dishes. Plan-ahead types can make the curd, cake, and caramel up to two days ahead (the curd needs at least a few hours to chill), then whip the cream right before assembling. DIY types can grind the almond flour fresh; if buying it, check the bulk bins if you don't want to invest in a whole bag.

9 large tangerines

POUND CAKE

½ cup (1 stick/115 g) unsalted butter, plus more for greasing
1½ cups (190 g) all-purpose flour
½ cup (60 g) almond flour, sifted
1 teaspoon baking powder
½ teaspoon kosher salt
¼ teaspoon baking soda
2 large eggs
⅔ cup (135 g) sugar
¾ cup (180 ml) plain full-fat Greek-style yogurt
1 teaspoon pure vanilla extract
½ teaspoon pure almond extract

CARAMEL

¼ cup (50 g) sugar
3 tablespoons fresh tangerine juice
1 tablespoon Cointreau

1. Zest all the tangerines with a Microplane grater. Set aside 1 tablespoon plus 2 teaspoons of the zest in a small bowl and freeze the rest for another use. Juice one of the tangerines and set aside 3 tablespoons of the juice for the caramel. Trim the ends off each remaining tangerine with a very sharp paring knife, then slice off all the remaining peel and pith. Slice the tangerines crosswise into ¼-inch-thick (6 mm) wheels and place them in a bowl.

2. To make the pound cake: Preheat the oven to 325°F (160°C). Butter an 8½-by-4½-inch (1.4 L) loaf pan, then line it with a strip of parchment paper, leaving a few inches (5 to 7.5 cm) overhanging on the long sides.

3. Melt the butter in a small saucepan over low heat, then let cool slightly. Whisk together the all-purpose flour, almond flour, baking powder, salt, and baking soda in a small bowl. Whisk together the eggs and sugar in a large bowl until smooth and pale yellow, about 1 minute. Stir in the yogurt, 1 tablespoon of the tangerine zest, the vanilla, and the almond extract. Slowly whisk in the melted butter until smooth. Add the dry ingredients to the wet ingredients and mix just until combined (the batter will be thick). Transfer the batter to the prepared pan and smooth the top. Bake until the cake is golden and springs back when you press on it, 50 to 55 minutes. Remove from the oven and let cool in the pan for 10 minutes, then transfer the cake to a wire rack and let cool completely.

WHIPPED CREAM

2 cups (480 ml) heavy cream

2 tablespoons sugar

1 teaspoon pure vanilla extract

1 teaspoon pure almond extract

1 recipe Tangerine Dream Curd (page 153)

AT THE CABIN

- **Microplane grater**
- **3-quart (3 L) trifle bowl**

4. While the cake is cooling, make the caramel: Combine the sugar and 2 tablespoons water in a small saucepan. Cook over medium heat, stirring, until the sugar has dissolved, then boil, without stirring, until the mixture is dark amber, 5 to 7 minutes. Remove from the heat and stir in the tangerine juice, Cointreau, and ½ teaspoon of the tangerine zest. Let cool completely.

5. To make the whipped cream: In the bowl of a stand mixer fitted with the whisk attachment, or in a large bowl with a handheld mixer, whip the cream, sugar, 1 teaspoon of the tangerine zest, the vanilla, and the almond extract. Cover and refrigerate until ready to use.

6. To assemble the trifle: Cut an inch (2.5 cm) off either end of the cake and save the pieces for breakfast. Cut the remaining cake into 6 equal slices, then cut each slice into 6 cubes and layer them in the bottom of a 3-quart (3 L) trifle bowl. Reserve a heaping cup (240 ml) of the whipped cream for garnish and spread the rest over the cake. Top with the tangerine slices, reserving some to press flat against the side of the dish (purely for aesthetic effect; see illustration). Layer the curd next, then mound the reserved whipped cream on top and pour the caramel over everything. Sprinkle the trifle with the remaining ½ teaspoon tangerine zest. Serve the trifle immediately, or cover and refrigerate it for up to 2 hours (let it sit out for 15 minutes before serving).

PBJ Skillet Brownie Sundae

SERVES 4 TO 6 (MAKES 1 CUP/240 ML OF EACH SAUCE)

This dessert-friendly take on the ever-popular lunch-sack stuffable warms cold winter nights in the form of a gooey brownie sundae topped with peanut butter hot fudge and strawberry sauce. Fresh strawberries are one of the easier fruits to find on grocery shelves year-round, but you can use frozen berries if need be; the sauce will still be scrumptious. If you have instant espresso, sprinkle a few spoonfuls into the brownie batter and hot fudge to make them even richer than a St. Moritz socialite.

BROWNIES

4 tablespoons (½ stick/60 g) unsalted butter, plus more for greasing

2 tablespoons neutral oil, such as vegetable, canola, or light olive oil

⅔ cup (65 g) unsweetened cocoa powder, sifted

½ cup (65 g) all-purpose flour

2 teaspoons instant espresso

½ teaspoon kosher salt

1 cup (200 g) sugar

2 large eggs

1 teaspoon pure vanilla extract

1. To make the brownies: Preheat the oven to 350°F (180°C). Melt together the butter and oil in an 8-inch (20 cm) cast-iron skillet over medium-low heat until very hot.

2. Sift together the cocoa powder and flour into a small bowl, then stir in the instant espresso and salt. Whisk together the sugar, eggs, and vanilla in a large bowl until smooth and pale yellow, about 2 minutes. Whisking continuously, slowly pour the hot butter mixture into the egg mixture and whisk until smooth, about 30 seconds. (Swipe any leftover butter mixture around the skillet to thoroughly grease it, adding more butter if necessary.)

3. Stir in the dry ingredients until just combined, then transfer the batter to the skillet. Bake the brownies until the top appears dry and crackly and the center is firm but still moist, about 23 minutes. (They'll keep baking in the skillet for a bit after they're removed from the oven.)

4. To make the peanut butter hot fudge: Combine the cream, peanut butter, chocolate, cocoa powder, sugar, corn syrup, instant espresso, vanilla, and salt in a small saucepan and heat over medium heat, stirring continuously, until hot, thick, glossy, and smooth. Let cool slightly before using. (If not using immediately, transfer to a widemouthed pint/480 ml jar, cover, and store in the refrigerator for up to 1 week; rewarm in a small saucepan before using.)

PEANUT BUTTER HOT FUDGE

½ cup (120 ml) heavy cream

⅓ cup (80 ml) creamy peanut butter

2 ounces (57 g) bittersweet chocolate, chopped, or chips (about ⅓ cup)

1 tablespoon unsweetened cocoa powder, sifted

2 tablespoons sugar

2 tablespoons light corn syrup

1 teaspoon instant espresso

1 teaspoon pure vanilla extract

⅛ teaspoon kosher salt

SEVEN-MINUTE STRAWBERRY SAUCE

1 pound (455 g) strawberries, hulled and quartered

¼ cup (50 g) sugar

2 teaspoons fresh lemon juice

¼ teaspoon pure vanilla extract

1 pint (473 ml) vanilla bean ice cream

¼ cup (60 ml) heavy cream, whipped

2 tablespoons coarsely chopped roasted salted peanuts

Sprinkles (optional, but always appreciated)

AT THE CABIN

- Immersion blender (optional)

5. To make the strawberry sauce: Combine the strawberries, sugar, lemon juice, and vanilla in a small saucepan. Bring to a boil over medium heat, then cook, stirring frequently, until thick and jammy, about 7 minutes. If you prefer the sauce smooth, not chunky, purée it in the saucepan with an immersion blender, or transfer it to a standing blender and purée. Let cool slightly before using. (If not using immediately, transfer to a widemouthed pint/480 ml jar, cover, and store in the refrigerator for up to 1 week; rewarm in a small saucepan before using.)

6. To assemble the brownie sundae: While the skillet brownie is still warm (but not hot, or the ice cream will instantly melt), scoop the ice cream on top, drizzle with warm peanut butter hot fudge and strawberry sauce, and top with the whipped cream, peanuts, and sprinkles (if using). Pass around spoons, and let the dessert delirium commence.

TINY TIP: *Not a strawberry to be found on the mountain? Warm up a cup (240 ml) of strawberry jam instead, thinning it with a tablespoon or two of water if necessary.*

Apple-Cranberry Strudel

SERVES 6 TO 8

We use mellow, creamy, easy-to-get Galas in this sweet-tart strudel, but any good baking apple will do (bump up the sugar a bit if you're a Granny Smith superfan). You can also try currants, raisins, dried cherries, or dried apricots in place of the cranberries. Ideally, serve the strudel with scoops of vanilla bean ice cream, although it's also delicious with Dark Rum Sauce (see page 160). Or whipped cream. Or plain. You really can't go wrong here.

½ cup (60 g) walnuts
1 pound (455 g) Gala apples, peeled, cored, and cut into ¼-inch (6 mm) slices
½ cup (70 g) dried cranberries
3 tablespoons sugar
2 tablespoons panko bread crumbs
¼ teaspoon grated lemon zest
1 teaspoon fresh lemon juice
½ teaspoon ground cinnamon
¼ teaspoon kosher salt
⅛ teaspoon freshly grated nutmeg
6 (13-by-18-inch/ 33 by 45 cm) sheets phyllo dough
4 tablespoons (½ stick/ 60 g) unsalted butter, melted
1 egg, beaten with 1 tablespoon milk, for egg wash
1 pint (473 ml) vanilla bean ice cream (optional)

AT THE CABIN
• Microplane grater

1. Preheat the oven to 375°F (190°C). Line a rimmed half sheet pan with parchment paper.

2. Cook the walnuts in a small skillet over medium-low heat, tossing occasionally (don't let them burn), until toasted, 5 to 7 minutes. Let cool slightly, then coarsely chop.

3. Mix together the apples, cranberries, sugar, panko, lemon zest, lemon juice, cinnamon, salt, nutmeg, and toasted walnuts in a large bowl.

4. Lay one sheet of phyllo on a piece of parchment paper or cutting board, with the long side parallel to you. (Cover the remaining sheets with a damp kitchen towel to keep them from drying out while you work.) Quickly brush the entire sheet with melted butter. Layer another phyllo sheet on top and brush it with butter. Continue until all six sheets are stacked and buttered.

5. Transfer the filling to the side of the phyllo closest to you, shaping it into a long, slim pile about 3 inches (8 cm) wide and leaving a 1½-inch (4 cm) border from the edges. Fold the left and right sides inward over the filling, then fold the closest long edge over the filling. Tuck any wayward filling in and roll the strudel burrito-style into a log (see the illustrations opposite).

1. Placing the filling

2. Folding the sides

3. Folding the edge

4. Cutting the diagonal slits

6. Transfer the strudel to the prepared sheet pan, seam-side down. Brush the top of the strudel generously with the egg wash. With a sharp paring knife, cut diagonal slits across the top, about 2 inches (5 cm) apart (like you're cutting slits in a piecrust). Bake the strudel until golden brown, about 35 minutes. Remove from the oven and let cool on the pan for 10 minutes, then slice and serve with scoops of vanilla bean ice cream, if desired.

TINY TIP: *If you have any Cider Syrup (see page 205) sitting around in the refrigerator, add a tablespoon or two to the strudel filling to deepen the apple flavor.*

Banana Tarte Tatin
with Dark Rum Sauce

SERVES 8

Swap apples for bananas in this twist on the classic tarte tatin, an upside-down tart hiding decadent, deeply caramelized fruit. Use bananas that are ripe but still firm, and be sure to pull your puff pastry out of the freezer or snowbank to thaw (preferably overnight in the refrigerator, or for about 45 minutes at room temperature) before you start.

TARTE TATIN

1 sheet frozen
  all-butter puff
  pastry, such as
  Dufour, thawed
All-purpose flour,
  for dusting
4 tablespoons (½ stick/
  60 g) unsalted
  butter
⅓ cup packed (75 g)
  light brown sugar
½ teaspoon ground
  cinnamon
¼ teaspoon kosher salt
4 large firm ripe
  bananas, cut on a
  slight angle into
  ¼-inch-thick (6 mm)
  slices

DARK RUM SAUCE

⅓ cup (80 ml) heavy
  cream
⅓ cup (80 ml) whole
  milk
2 large egg yolks
2 tablespoons sugar
⅛ teaspoon kosher salt
Pinch of freshly grated
  nutmeg
1 tablespoon dark
  spiced rum, such as
  Kraken
¼ teaspoon pure
  vanilla extract

1. To make the tarte tatin: Preheat the oven to 400°F (200°C).

2. Roll out the puff pastry on a lightly floured surface into a 10-inch (25 cm) square (or slice off one of the ends and patch it into a square). Invert a 10-inch (25 cm) ovenproof skillet on top of the pastry and use it as a guide to trace and cut a round of pastry. Transfer the round to the plate or platter on which you plan to serve the tarte tatin (find one that's at least 1 inch/ 2.5 cm wider in diameter than the skillet, for easier flipping later) and refrigerate until needed.

3. In the same skillet, melt the butter over medium heat. Add the brown sugar, cinnamon, and salt and stir until the mixture is smooth and bubbling, about 2 minutes. Remove the pan from the heat and layer the bananas in concentric circles on top of the brown sugar mixture. Retrieve the puff pastry round from the refrigerator and set it on top of the bananas. Bake until the puff pastry is, in fact, puffy and golden brown, and the filling is bubbling merrily at the edges, 25 to 30 minutes.

4. While the tarte tatin is baking, make the rum sauce: Heat the cream and milk in a small saucepan over medium heat until not quite simmering, then remove from the heat. Whisk the egg yolks, sugar, salt, and nutmeg in a small bowl until pale yellow and smooth, about 1 minute. While whisking continuously, slowly pour the hot cream mixture into the yolk mixture in a thin stream to temper the yolks. Pour everything back into the saucepan and heat over medium heat, stirring continuously, until the sauce reaches 160°F (71°C), 2 to 3 minutes (don't let it get too hot, or the custard will curdle). Remove from the heat and stir in the rum and vanilla.

5. When the tarte tatin is finished baking, remove it from the oven, let cool for 5 minutes, then place a serving platter over the skillet and quickly and *very* carefully (wear hot pads!) invert them together and remove the pan (the bananas will be faceup). Let the tarte tatin cool slightly, then cut it into 8 wedges and drizzle each with 1 tablespoon of rum sauce. Serve with the rest of the sauce alongside.

TINY TIP: *If you don't have the ingredients or the will to make the rum sauce, simply melt 1 cup (240 ml) good-quality vanilla bean ice cream in a small saucepan and heat until warmed, punch it up with rum to taste, and proceed. If even that seems like overexertion, plop scoops of ice cream on top of each slice of tarte tatin (splash of rum optional).*

Burnt Honey and Thyme Roasted Pears

SERVES 4

Use pears that hold their shape when baked, like Anjou, Bartlett, or Bosc, and choose ones that are just short of being fully ripe, so they don't turn to mush in the oven. If your pears are wobbly and watching the honey slide off them aggravates your type A streak, slice a bit off the bottom of each half so they stay level on the pan; it will look funny when you flip them the first time, but once they're in the bowl, nobody will ever know. The honey that dribbles onto the sheet pan will bubble and burn slightly during baking; while perhaps initially alarming, this adds rich flavor to the pan juices.

4 large pears
  (see headnote)
4 tablespoons
  (½ stick/60 g)
  unsalted butter,
  cut into 8 cubes
½ cup (120 ml) honey
2 teaspoons chopped
  fresh thyme, plus
  8 small sprigs
Flaky sea salt
½ cup (120 ml) heavy
  cream

AT THE CABIN
• **Melon baller**

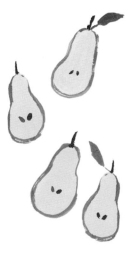

1. Preheat the oven to 400°F (200°C). Line a rimmed half sheet pan with parchment paper (cover the entire pan, even up the sides, to make cleanup easier).

2. Cut each pear in half lengthwise and core it with a melon baller. Place the pears cut-side up on the prepared sheet pan and place a cube of butter inside each half. Drizzle 1 tablespoon of honey inside and over each half, sprinkle each with ¼ teaspoon of the chopped thyme and a pinch of flaky salt, and top with a thyme sprig.

3. Bake the pears for 15 minutes, then remove the sheet pan from the oven, gently flip the pears over with tongs, swirl them around to coat them in the pan juices, and bake for 15 minutes more, until soft and starting to caramelize. Poke the pears with a fork; if they're still firm, flip them again, baste them with pan juices, and roast for 5 to 10 minutes more. Remove the pears from the oven and let cool for a few minutes on the pan.

4. Divide the heavy cream among four bowls. Place two pear halves in each bowl, then drizzle the pan juices over the top, dividing them evenly among the bowls. Top each pear half with a roasted thyme sprig and serve.

Calvados Apple Cake with Cinnamon Crème Fraîche

SERVES 8

This single-layer brandy-spiked French apple cake works well as a catching-up treat, the sort of thing that's nice to have around if a friend stops by or a relative is visiting and you want to offer them something to eat with their coffee. That said, the cake's small scale (easily polished off by a group) and amiability (skip the almond paste or the topping, and it'll still work out great) make it a welcome houseguest any day. Plus, it smells amazing while baking.

TOPPING

½ cup (120 ml) crème fraîche or yogurt
3 tablespoons confectioners' sugar
1 teaspoon ground cinnamon

CAKE

½ cup (1 stick/115 g) unsalted butter, cut into cubes, at room temperature, plus more for greasing
1 cup (125 g) all-purpose flour, plus more for dusting
1½ teaspoons baking powder
½ teaspoon kosher salt
1 cup (200 g) granulated sugar
3½ ounces (100 g) almond paste (see Tiny Tip)
1 teaspoon pure vanilla extract
2 tablespoons calvados or other apple brandy
3 large eggs
2 sweet-tart red apples, such as Fuji, Gala, or Pink Lady
Confectioners' sugar, for dusting

1. To make the topping: Whisk together the crème fraîche, confectioners' sugar, and cinnamon in a small bowl. Cover and refrigerate while you make the cake.

2. To make the cake: Position a rack in the center of the oven and preheat the oven to 350°F (180°C). Generously butter a 9-inch (23 cm) round cake pan and dust it with flour, tapping out any excess.

3. Whisk together the flour, baking powder, and salt in a large bowl. Combine the granulated sugar and almond paste in a food processor and process until finely ground. Add the butter, vanilla, and calvados and process until smooth. Add the eggs one at a time and process for 3 minutes, scraping down the sides of the bowl at least once, until smooth and pale yellow. Pour the wet ingredients into the dry ingredients and stir with a nonstick spatula until the dry ingredients are just incorporated.

4. Scrape the batter into the prepared pan. Thinly slice the apples and arrange the slices in a circle on top of the cake, working from the outside in. Bake for 1 hour, or until the cake is golden brown and set when you press the top with your finger. Dust with confectioners' sugar and serve each slice with a dollop of the topping.

TINY TIP: *The speediest way to break down almond paste is in the food processor, but if you don't have one, a stand mixer (fitted with the paddle attachment) plus a bit more dedication (time + scraping the sides of the bowl) will do.*

Can't Catch Me Gingerbread Cakes with Candied Kumquats

MAKES 6 MINI CAKES

Our trio of pint-size recipe testers report that mini gingerbread cakes baked in a 6-cup muffin tin offer optimal glaze-to-cake ratio. (You could also bake this gingerbread in a 9-inch/23 cm cake pan, or double the batter to bake it in a Bundt pan.) To ward off the anxiety of leaving half the cake in the pan, line the bottom of each mega-muffin-tin cup with a circle of parchment paper. It may be overkill, but it's failproof. To make the circles, look for a mug, prep bowl, or bottom of a sriracha bottle that matches the bottom of the muffin tin, trace six circles on parchment paper, and recruit your little sous chefs to practice their scissor skills.

CANDIED KUMQUATS
1 cup (200 g) sugar
20 kumquats, sliced into ⅛-inch-thick (3 mm) wheels and seeded (see Tiny Tips)

CAKE
Nonstick cooking spray
1¼ cups (160 g) all-purpose flour
2 teaspoons unsweetened cocoa powder
½ teaspoon baking powder
¼ teaspoon kosher salt
⅛ teaspoon baking soda
2 teaspoons ground ginger
1 teaspoon ground cinnamon
¼ teaspoon ground cloves
¼ teaspoon freshly grated nutmeg
6 tablespoons (¾ stick/85 g) unsalted butter, cut into cubes, at room temperature

1. To make the candied kumquats: Bring the sugar and ¾ cup (180 ml) water to a gentle simmer in a small pot, stirring frequently until the sugar has dissolved and the syrup is clear. Add the kumquats and simmer over low heat for 10 minutes, spooning the syrup over the kumquats to cover. Transfer the kumquats and syrup to a jar. (If not using immediately, store in an airtight container in the refrigerator for up to 1 month.)

2. To make the cake: Position a rack in the center of the oven and preheat the oven to 350°F (180°C). Spray a 6-cup muffin tin with nonstick spray, line the cups with parchment paper, then lightly spray the parchment.

3. In a medium bowl, whisk together the flour, cocoa powder, baking powder, salt, baking soda, and spices (see Tiny Tips).

4. Cream the butter and brown sugar in the bowl of a stand mixer fitted with the paddle attachment for 5 minutes, stopping and scraping down the sides of the bowl at least once. One at a time, add the egg, the molasses, coffee, ½ cup (120 ml) water, and vanilla, mixing until combined after each addition before adding the next. (The batter may break and look funky at this moment. Don't be nervous.) Add the dry ingredients in two portions and mix just until incorporated.

¾ cup packed (165 g) dark brown sugar

1 egg, at room temperature

¼ cup (60 ml) unsulfured molasses (not blackstrap)

¼ cup (60 ml) brewed coffee, cooled

½ teaspoon pure vanilla extract

Confectioners' sugar, for dusting

GLAZE

1 cup (125 g) confectioners' sugar

1 tablespoon fresh orange juice, strained of pulp

1 teaspoon fresh lemon juice

5. Evenly divide the batter among the prepared muffin cups and smooth the tops. Bake for 30 minutes, until a toothpick inserted into the center comes out clean and the cakes are springy. Let cool in the pan on a wire rack, then run a knife inside the muffin cups to loosen any stuck bits. Set the rack on a sheet pan and invert the pan onto the rack. (Cool completely, or the glaze won't stay put.)

6. To make the glaze: Sift the confectioners' sugar into a medium bowl. Whisk in the orange juice and lemon juice until smooth. Spoon the glaze over the tops of the cakes, allowing the glaze to drip down the sides. Let set.

7. Transfer the cakes to dessert plates and top each with a spoonful of the candied kumquats.

TINY TIPS: *If you're having trouble thinly slicing your kumquats, try using a serrated knife. Extra kumquat syrup can be used to sweeten cocktails or seltzer, or drizzled on French toast.*

If you're looking to shorten your shopping list, you can substitute 2 tablespoons premixed gingerbread spice for the ginger, cinnamon, cloves, and nutmeg called for in this recipe.

CHAPTER 6

Fortifications

While everyone knows you don't need liquor to have a good time, it certainly can help, especially when the temperature is almost arctic enough to freeze vodka. This chapter pours out seasonally driven sips of all persuasions; from a zero-proof Grapefruit-Rosemary Spritzer and Hot Chocolate Hodgepodge to post-snow-day pick-me-ups like sweet and sassy Whiskey Cider, maple-syrup-spiked Yuzu Sour, and a trio of sherry cocktails. Since a quality collection of nightcaps is a must on a snowy sojourn, be sure to cap your cold day with a hot drink, like a green-apple-peel-infused calvados toddy, delightfully Boozy Orange Bourbon Eggnog, or hygge-inducing Scandinavian-style Cranberry-Cardamom Glogg. If no nightcap is necessary because you're staying up until the lifts reopen, grab the schnapps and head straight for the Shotski, Why Can't We Quit Thee? tutorial.

Hail(storm) Caesar

MAKES 1

Canada's national cocktail is a briny twist on the classic Bloody Mary. There are as many variations on it as there are tuques in the lost-and-found at Whistler Blackcomb; however, the most authentic version is made with Montreal Steak Seasoning and Mott's Clamato. If you can't find those exact brands at the grocery store, fear not—your Canadian friends are way too nice to criticize your cocktail anyway. Swap in 1½ teaspoons kosher salt and ½ teaspoon freshly ground black pepper for the steak seasoning and another (undoubtedly inferior) clam-based tomato juice for the Clamato.

1 teaspoon Montreal Steak Seasoning
2 pinches of celery salt
Lemon wedge
4 ounces (120 ml) Mott's Clamato
2 ounces (60 ml) vodka
½ ounce (15 ml) fresh lemon juice
¼ ounce (7 ml) Worcestershire sauce
2 dashes of Tabasco sauce
Pinch of freshly ground black pepper
1 pickled green bean, for garnish
2 pitted green olives, for garnish
1 tiny cherry tomato, for garnish
Tiny Canadian flag, for garnish (optional)

1. Mix the steak seasoning and one pinch of the celery salt in a saucer. Rub the lemon wedge around the rim of a highball glass, then invert the glass into the saucer to coat the rim.

2. Combine the Mott's Clamato, vodka, lemon juice, Worcestershire, Tabasco, remaining pinch of celery salt, and the pepper in a cocktail shaker. Add ice and shake for 30 seconds. Strain into the rimmed highball glass. Use a cocktail pick to spear one end of the pickled green bean, then an olive, the tomato, another olive, and finally the other end of the green bean, then garnish the glass. Or garnish with a lemon wedge and a tiny Canadian flag.

TINY TIP: *Kick things up by infusing your vodka with fresh horseradish root. Pour off (and reserve!) 1 cup (240 ml) vodka from a 750 ml bottle. Peel a 4-inch (10 cm) segment of fresh horseradish root, slice it into coins, drop them into the bottle, and put on the top. Steep the horseradish vodka for 1 week, then start mixing the Caesars. Strain the vodka and transfer to a clean bottle or container to maintain the flavor, or continue steeping, if you like it super spicy.*

Bartender's Refresher: Five Essential Winter Cocktails

When a snowstorm knocks out the Wi-Fi, know how to make these five classic cocktails by heart. Each recipe makes one drink.

1. MARTINI

2½ ounces (75 ml) gin
½ ounce (15 ml) dry vermouth
Lemon peel

Stir the gin and vermouth in an ice-filled mixing glass for 30 seconds until chilled. Strain into a chilled coupe. Garnish with the lemon peel.

2. MANHATTAN

2 ounces (60 ml) rye whiskey or bourbon
1 ounce (30 ml) sweet vermouth
2 dashes of bitters
Maraschino cherry, preferably Luxardo

Stir the whiskey, vermouth, and bitters in an ice-filled mixing glass for 30 seconds until chilled. Strain into a chilled coupe. Garnish with the cherry.

3. BOULEVARDIER

1½ ounces (45 ml) bourbon
¾ ounce (22 ml) sweet vermouth
¾ ounce (22 ml) Campari
Orange peel

Stir the bourbon, vermouth, and Campari in an ice-filled mixing glass for 30 seconds until chilled. Strain into a chilled coupe. Garnish with the orange peel.

4. WHITE RUSSIAN

1½ ounces (45 ml) vodka
¾ ounce (22 ml) coffee liqueur
¾ ounce (22 ml) heavy cream

Combine the vodka, coffee liqueur, and cream in an ice-filled shaker and shake for 30 seconds until chilled. Strain into a tumbler.

5. MOSCOW MULE

2 ounces (60 ml) vodka
½ ounce (15 ml) fresh lime juice
6 ounces (180 ml) ginger beer, preferably Fever-Tree or Fentimans
Lime wedge

Stir the vodka and lime in a copper mug filled halfway with ice for 30 seconds until chilled. Top with the ginger beer. Garnish with the lime wedge.

Sherry Baby

Sherry, that much-maligned fortified wine, was once cast aside in America as a too-sweet treat for the senior set. In recent years, it's found its footing as a food-friendly sipper that won't set you back. With a chilled bottle of sherry on hand, you're never more than a pour away from an elegant kickoff to your fireside bites.

All sherries start in southern Spain, in what's known as the "sherry triangle" between Jerez de la Frontera, El Puerto de Santa María, and Sanlúcar de Barrameda. Yet the range of styles that come from those same green grapes is extraordinary—from a pale fino so drinkable you could easily polish off the bottle to a rich Pedro Ximénez (PX) that's a dessert unto itself. If your only impression of sherry is sickly sweet cream sherry, which can vary widely in quality, shake it off and start fresh. Pick up a dry fino or manzanilla sherry, which drinks like a chilled wine (once it's opened, drink it within a week) and pairs well with a salty nut mix or potato chips. Briny and crisp, a classic Bamboo (recipe follows), the martini of the sherry world, showcases it well. Once you've gotten to know fino, venture into nutty amontillado; a super sipper as well as a splendid cocktail component for a Cobbler (recipe follows). Now venture to the darker hues. Aromatic oloroso makes for an excellent cocktail component, offering depth and richness to round out aged mezcal in our Snowed In (recipe follows). Each recipe makes one drink.

BAMBOO

1½ ounces (45 ml) fino sherry
1½ ounces (45 ml) dry vermouth
2 dashes of orange bitters
1 dash of Angostura bitters
1 (3-inch/8 cm) strip grapefruit peel

Combine the sherry, vermouth, and bitters in a mixing glass filled with ice. Stir for 30 seconds until chilled. Strain into a chilled coupe. Express the grapefruit peel's oils over the drink, then drop it into the glass.

COBBLER

3 ounces (90 ml) amontillado
  sherry
½ ounce (15 ml) fresh orange
  juice
½ ounce (15 ml) Demerara syrup
Orange slice
Mint sprig

Combine the sherry, orange juice, and Demerara syrup in a mixing glass filled with ice. Stir for 30 seconds until chilled. Strain into a highball glass filled with crushed ice. Garnish with the orange slice and mint.

SNOWED IN

2 ounces (60 ml) mezcal
1 ounce (30 ml) oloroso sherry
1 ounce (30 ml) fresh grapefruit juice
½ ounce (15 ml) fresh lemon juice
½ ounce (15 ml) Demerara syrup
1 (3-inch/8 cm) lemon twist

Combine the mezcal, sherry, grapefruit juice, lemon juice, and Demerara syrup in a mixing glass filled with ice. Stir for 30 seconds until chilled. Strain into a chilled coupe. Garnish with the lemon twist.

Cranberry Margaritas for a Crowd

MAKES 1 PITCHER

This tart tipple makes the perfect pitcher for your next holiday party because, like Christmas in July (only the other way around), it's an off-season favorite returning with a festive twist. Shop for unsweetened cranberry juice and 100% agave tequila.

2 cups (480 ml)
blanco tequila
2 cups (480 ml)
cranberry juice
(not cranberry
cocktail)
1½ cups (360 ml)
Cointreau or
triple sec
½ cup (120 ml) fresh
lime juice
Fresh cranberries,
for garnish
Rosemary sprigs,
for garnish
Blood orange wheels,
for garnish
2 tablespoons kosher
salt
2 tablespoons sugar
Lime wedges

1. Combine the tequila, cranberry juice, Cointreau, and lime juice in an ice-filled pitcher and stir. (If not serving immediately, omit the ice and chill the base in the refrigerator for up to 1 day.) Garnish the pitcher with any or all of the following: cranberries, rosemary sprigs, and blood orange wheels. Let stand for at least 5 minutes to chill.

2. Meanwhile, combine the salt and sugar on a saucer. Run a lime wedge along the rim of just one side of a tumbler, then lightly roll that portion of the rim in the salt-sugar mixture to make a half-moon. Repeat with three additional tumblers.

3. Fill the glasses halfway with ice and a few cranberries. Pour in the margarita and garnish with a lime wedge.

TINY TIP: *If this margarita is too sassy for your taste, and maybe it's dawning on you that years of vodka-cranberries have inured you to a more cloying cranberry cocktail, fear not! It's simple enough to sweeten your pitcher, all while adding a note of holiday spice. Bring ½ cup (120 ml) water, ½ cup (100 g) sugar, and 2 cinnamon sticks to a gentle simmer in a small pot, stirring until the sugar has dissolved and the syrup is clear. Remove from the heat and steep, ideally overnight or for at least 1 hour (or, what the hay, just 5 minutes, if you've already mixed the pitcher). Remove the cinnamon sticks and stir 2 tablespoons of the syrup into the pitcher at a time, tasting after each addition.*

Shotski, Why Can't We Quit Thee?

All hail the bar mitzvah hype dancer of après-ski culture: love it or hate it, there's no chance you'll escape it.

Origin Story

Whoever the mad genius was who first decided to mount three to five shot glasses to a discarded ski, fill them with booze, and invite friends to imbibe in complete synchronicity is lost to history. We like to think it was Ernest Hemingway, during his Sun Valley years, but that vainglorious powder hound would have certainly insisted on being photographed while doing it. (As should you.)

DIY

Shotskis are made, not born. To make yours, measure twice and drill once: measure the center of the ski crosswise and every 18 inches (45 cm) lengthwise to mark the placement of the shot glasses. Wearing protective eyewear and a mask, because shotski making is serious business, drill to the core of the ski using a 1⅜-inch (3.5 cm) Forstner drill bit. Glue four plastic shot glasses in place with clear adhesive. Or, for easier cleaning, attach the shot glasses with Velcro or a circular magnet and a washer.

Good Form

Set up for success by evaluating the height of all participants. Encourage the tall folks to scrunch down a bit and the small folks to stand on tiptoe, and tap a neutral third party (not the bartender—she's busy) to count down from 3.

Spirits of Competition

In the battle for longest shotski, two stellar ski towns—Breckenridge, Colorado, and Park City, Utah—are locked in stiff competition. As of this writing, Park City holds the record. In 2019, 1,300 people downed shots from a 2,610-foot-long (795 m) shotski.

Schnappski

Jägermeister, that oft-ordered shotski shooter, is also a digestif, as is its herbally obsessed Czech cousin, Becherovka. At 70+ proof, however, it's a commitment. For half the headache, do as they do in Austria, and turn down the volume by ordering (30 proof) schnapps shots for the ski instead.

Skipski

By design, the shotski disallows the possibility of discreetly pouring your Fireball into a nearby potted plant. However, even in official record-setting competitions (see Park City, above), it's regulation rules to substitute apple juice and still be very much a part of the team.

Whiskey Cider

MAKES 1

Rich, fresh-pressed apple cider plus whiskey—what could go wrong? Actually, don't ask, and also, no, we have never ever made a naked snow angel. If you just did, and thus require more of a winter warmer than cooler, heat the apple cider and whiskey in a small saucepan until hot and skip the ice.

½ cup (120 ml)
  unfiltered apple
  cider (see Tiny Tip)
1½ ounces (45 ml)
  whiskey
1 (3-inch/8 cm) strip
  lemon peel
1 cinnamon stick,
  for garnish

Stir together the apple cider and whiskey in a tumbler filled with ice. Express the lemon peel's oils over the drink, then drop it into the glass. Garnish with the cinnamon stick and serve.

TINY TIP: *If your cider press is out of order, make ½ cup (120 ml) fresh-pressed cider on the spot by juicing two medium Gala or Fuji apples in a juicer.*

Boozy Orange Bourbon Eggnog

SERVES 4

Yes, those festive red-and-green holiday cartons are tempting, but making your own eggnog is as easy as yoonering and far more delicious. As a bonus, when you get a 'nog craving in the middle of August (hey, it happens), you're covered. If you don't have both rum and bourbon, just double up on whichever one you have.

Zest of 1 large orange,
   removed in 1-inch
   (2.5 cm) strips
1½ cups (360 ml)
   whole milk
1½ cups (360 ml)
   heavy cream
6 large egg yolks
⅓ cup (65 g) sugar
⅛ teaspoon kosher salt
½ teaspoon ground
   nutmeg, plus more
   for garnish
½ teaspoon pure
   vanilla extract
¼ cup (60 ml) dark
   spiced rum, such as
   Kraken
¼ cup (60 ml) bourbon

1. Combine the orange peels, milk, and cream in a medium lidded saucepan. Bring to a simmer over medium heat, then remove from the heat, cover, and let steep for 30 minutes.

2. Remove the peels from the saucepan. Rinse and pat dry four for garnish and discard the rest. Bring the milk mixture back to a simmer over medium heat. Whisk together the egg yolks, sugar, and salt in a large bowl until pale yellow and smooth, about 1 minute. Whisking continuously, slowly pour the hot milk mixture into the yolk mixture in a thin stream to temper the yolks.

3. Pour everything back into the saucepan and cook over medium heat, whisking continuously, until the mixture reaches 160°F (71°C), 2 to 3 minutes (don't let it get too hot, or the custard will curdle). Remove from the heat.

4. Stir in the nutmeg, vanilla, rum, and bourbon, then refrigerate the eggnog until chilled. (Or serve it warm—it's still delicious, and there's no wait!)

5. Divide the eggnog among four glasses and sprinkle more nutmeg on top. Express the oils from one of the reserved orange peels over each drink, then drop it into the glass. The eggnog will keep in an airtight container in the refrigerator for up to 5 days.

TINY TIP: *To make eggnog custard, skip step 3, reduce the rum and bourbon to 1 tablespoon each, divide the eggnog among six 8-ounce (240 ml) ramekins, set inside a glass baking dish, fill with hot water up to the level of the custard, and bake at 350°F (180°C) until set but still slightly jiggly, 40 to 45 minutes (tent with foil toward the end if the custards are getting too brown on top).*

Cranberry-Cardamom Glogg

SERVES 4

Glogg, mulled wine's Scandinavian sister, is a drink and a dessert all in one, thanks to the dried fruit and nuts at the bottom of the glass. Since you're infusing the wine with honey and spice and everything nice, there's no need to break out the bottle of 1947 Cheval Blanc you've been saving for when you win the World Snowshoe Championships—just pick up a reasonably priced dry, fruity red at the market. If you don't like your glogg *too* boozy, start with half the cranberry liqueur and akvavit, then add more to taste.

1 (750 ml) bottle red wine
¼ cup (60 ml) honey
8 green cardamom pods, cracked
8 whole black peppercorns
1 (3-inch/8 cm) cinnamon stick
4 (1½-inch/4 cm) slices fresh ginger
8 whole cloves
4 (1-by-3-inch/ 2.5 by 8 cm) strips orange peel
⅓ cup (80 ml) cranberry liqueur, such as Stone Barn Brandyworks (see Pantry Provisions, page 218)
¼ cup (60 ml) akvavit
¼ cup (35 g) dried cranberries
¼ cup (30 g) slivered almonds

1. Combine the wine, honey, cardamom pods, peppercorns, cinnamon stick, and ginger in a large saucepan over medium-low heat. Poke 2 cloves into each strip of orange peel and add the peels to the saucepan. Bring the mixture to a simmer, then reduce the heat to low, cover, and simmer very gently for 10 minutes. Remove from the heat and let steep for 30 minutes to 1 hour.

2. Bring the wine back to a simmer (unless it's still hot enough for you), then remove from the heat. Add the cranberry liqueur, akvavit, dried cranberries, and almonds and let sit for 5 minutes. Strain the glogg through a fine-mesh sieve into a 1-quart (1 L) spouted glass measuring cup, reserving all the spices, cranberries, and almonds.

3. Divide the glogg among four glasses or mugs. Divide the cranberries and almonds between the glasses, then divide the ginger, orange zest, and spices among the glasses as garnish. Add the cinnamon stick to your favorite person's glass, settle the ensuing squabble, and serve the glogg with small spoons for eating the cranberries and almonds.

Grapefruit-Rosemary Spritzer

MAKES 1

Born from the holy union of an accidentally doubled winter grapefruit box order and a generous neighbor's remarkably robust rosemary bushes, this refreshing zero-proof sparkler will afford both good (-tasting) company and a clear head while you're curled up by the cabin fire. The recipe makes enough honey-rosemary syrup for 8 drinks; or use the extra to sweeten hot tea.

¼ cup (60 ml) honey
3 (5-inch/12.5 cm) sprigs rosemary, plus 1 sprig for garnish
3 ounces (90 ml) fresh grapefruit juice, strained
4 ounces (120 ml) club soda

1. Stir together the honey and ¼ cup (60 ml) water in a small saucepan. Add 3 of the rosemary sprigs, crushing them slightly with your fingers to release their oils. Bring the syrup to a simmer over medium heat. Simmer for 30 seconds, then remove from the heat and let steep for 30 minutes. Discard the rosemary, pour the syrup into a 4-ounce (120 ml) mason jar, and refrigerate until chilled. (The syrup can be refrigerated for up to 1 month.)

2. Stir together 1 tablespoon of the honey-rosemary syrup and the grapefruit juice in a glass. Fill the glass with ice, then add the club soda and stir. Garnish with the remaining rosemary sprig and serve.

Blood Orange Negroni

MAKES 1

We've had some of our best Italian après-ski bar conversations after a couple of these fresh-blood-orange-juice-spiked Negronis, and we don't even speak Italian. Just kidding, but these are so easy to drink, don't blame us if you're the life of the Dinner in the Dolomites party (see page 152). If you can't find fresh blood oranges, look for bottled blood orange juice, or just use good old navels.

2 ounces (60 ml) fresh blood orange juice (from 1 orange), strained
1 ounce (30 ml) gin
1 ounce (30 ml) Campari
1 ounce (30 ml) sweet vermouth
Half-moon slice of blood orange

Combine the blood orange juice, gin, Campari, and vermouth in a cocktail shaker or glass filled with ice and stir until icy cold. Strain into a glass filled with ice and garnish with the blood orange slice.

Fizz the Season:
Five Fabulous Champagne Cocktails

Whether you're ringing in the new year in a snowbound Chamonix château, hosting a hang-loose holiday shindig in Heavenly, toasting a winter wedding in Whitefish, or just celebrating not getting caught behind the snowplow on your way up the mountain, we have something sparkly for you. You can of course use bona fide Champagne to craft these fun and festive sippers, but they're just as quaffable when made with more budget-friendly Prosecco, cava, or crémant.

---

1. POM WOW

1 ounce (30 ml) chilled
    pomegranate juice
½ teaspoon Cointreau
4 ounces (120 ml)
    champagne
1 tablespoon
    pomegranate arils,
    for garnish

Combine the pomegranate juice and Cointreau in a champagne glass. Add the champagne, then gently spoon the pomegranate arils on top so they float prettily.

---

2. GRAPEFRUIT HONEY FIZZ

3 (1-by-3-inch/
    2.5 by 8 cm) strips
    grapefruit peel
1½ ounces (45 ml)
    fresh Ruby Red
    grapefruit juice,
    strained
¾ ounce (22 ml) vodka
¾ teaspoon honey
    syrup (see Tiny Tip)
3 ounces (90 ml)
    champagne

Roll one grapefruit peel into a tight spiral, then wrap the remaining peels around it to form a "rose" and skewer it in place with a cocktail pick; set aside. Combine the grapefruit juice, vodka, and honey syrup in a cocktail shaker, fill with ice, and shake energetically for 15 seconds. Strain into a champagne glass. Add the champagne, then garnish with the grapefruit peel rose.

TINY TIP: *To make a quick batch of honey syrup, combine 1 part hot water and 1 part honey in a jar, screw the lid on tightly, and shake until completely combined.*

3. PASSIONFLOWER

½ ounce (15 ml) gin
½ ounce (15 ml)
  passion fruit purée,
  such as Boiron
½ ounce (15 ml)
  elderflower liqueur,
  such as St-Germain
4 ounces (120 ml)
  champagne
Sprig of elderflowers
  and/or spoonful of
  fresh passion fruit
  pulp

Combine the gin, passion fruit purée, and elderflower liqueur in a cocktail shaker, fill with ice, and shake energetically for 15 seconds. Strain into a champagne glass. Add the champagne, then garnish with elderflowers and/or passion fruit pulp.

4. RASPBERRY ROSE ROYALE

½ ounce (15 ml)
  Chambord
⅛ teaspoon rose water
5 ounces (150 ml)
  champagne or
  sparkling rosé
1 fresh raspberry and
  spray rose, speared
  on a cocktail pick

Combine the Chambord and rose water in a champagne glass. Add the champagne or sparkling rosé, then garnish with the raspberry rose cocktail pick.

5. GINGER 75

¾ ounce (22 ml)
  cognac
½ ounce (15 ml) Ginger
  Syrup (see Tiny Tip)
½ ounce (15 ml) fresh
  lemon juice
4 ounces (120 ml)
  champagne
1 (⅛-inch-thick/3 mm)
  cross section of
  ginger or a piece
  of candied ginger,
  speared on a cocktail
  pick

Combine the cognac, ginger syrup, and lemon juice in a cocktail shaker, fill with ice, and shake energetically for 15 seconds. Strain into a champagne glass. Add the champagne, then garnish with the ginger cross section or candied ginger pick.

TINY TIP: *To make ginger syrup, gently simmer ½ cup (100 g) sugar, ½ cup (120 ml) water, and ⅓ cup (35 g) grated ginger in a small saucepan for 5 minutes. Remove from the heat, let steep 1 hour, strain, and store in the refrigerator up to 1 month.*

A Winter's Ale: Porters, Stouts, and Other Dark Beers

When the snow flurries blow, let the ale flow—for expert advice on exactly *which* ales, we turned to brilliant beer buff Lucy Burningham, certified cicerone and author of *My Beer Year*. Here's her sage advice on how to ward off winter's chill with toasty porters, stouts, and other brrr-busting brews.

Dark and Stormy Flight

'Tis the season for drinking beers that look like winter's long nights—inky, obsidian-hued ales and lagers with delicious roasty notes. Don't let the color of these beers fool you: just because a beer is dark doesn't mean it's heavy or boozy. A beer's color comes from its malt: the more the grains are roasted, the darker the beer. But dark beers run the gamut in flavors and textures, from light and silky oatmeal stouts to rich, bourbon-barrel-aged porters. That means there's a dark beer for every food, from cheese to chocolate and everything in between.

Porters and Stouts

These closely intertwined English ales are nearly indistinguishable from each other today, and they share some of the best characteristics: notes of coffee and milk chocolate, and varying degrees of caramel sweetness. Oatmeal stouts are creamier and fuller, which makes them ideal for pairing with strong cheeses, while porters work well alongside smoked meats, rich stews, and charcuterie.

Imperial Stouts and Baltic Porters

These robust, complex sippers look stunning when served in snifters near a crackling fire. They're beautifully amped-up versions of stouts and porters, with flavors of coffee, dark chocolate, cocoa, dried fruit, and even leather and tobacco, which accompany higher alcohol content. Try imperial stouts with prime rib, pungent blue cheeses, and smoked Gouda. Sweeter Baltic porters pair well with mole sauces, roasted sausages, and butterscotch pudding.

German Lagers

The German tradition of making beers with just four ingredients (malt, hops, yeast, and water) produces a beautiful range of dark lagers. Look for the darkest of all the German lagers, schwarzbier ("black beer"), which, belying its foreboding hue, is easy drinking and lower in alcohol. On the other hand, doppelbocks, which were originally brewed to sustain monks while they fasted, are like a chewy, dense rye bread with notes of dried fruit and molasses. Indulge in this sipper alongside braised meats, gingerbread, and dark chocolate.

Yuzu à Deux:
Yuzu Sour and Yuzu Sake Toddy

You've fought over the cabin thermostat, exactly how much the window needs to be cracked to let in fresh air, and how many electric blankets should be on the bed (at least three); don't argue over what to drink. Here's an icy-cold whiskey sour and a cozy hot toddy, both made with yuzu—a versatile, uniquely flavorful tart-sour citrus fruit that's especially popular in Japan. If you can't source it fresh, use bottled yuzu juice, easily found at your local Asian market or online. Each recipe makes one cocktail.

YUZU SOUR

2 ounces (60 ml) bourbon
½ ounce (15 ml) fresh or bottled
   yuzu juice
½ ounce (15 ml) fresh lemon juice
¾ ounce (22 ml) pure maple syrup
1 (1-by-3-inch/2.5 by 8 cm) strip
   lemon peel

Combine the bourbon, yuzu juice, lemon juice, and maple syrup in a cocktail shaker, fill with ice, and shake energetically for 30 seconds. Strain the sour into a chilled coupe (or a tumbler filled with ice if you prefer it on the rocks). Garnish with the lemon peel.

YUZU SAKE TODDY

1 ounce (30 ml) fresh or bottled
   yuzu juice
2 ounces (60 ml) sake
1 jasmine green tea bag
6 ounces (180 ml) hot water
   (about 176°F/80°C)
1 tablespoon honey
1 (⅛-by-1½-inch/3 mm by 4 cm)
   slice fresh ginger
Slice of lemon

Warm the yuzu juice and sake in a small saucepan over low heat. Place the tea bag in a mug and pour the hot water over it. Let the tea steep for 4 minutes, then remove the bag and save it for a future cup of tea or discard it. Stir in the honey until completely dissolved. Stir in the yuzu juice and sake. Add the ginger and lemon slice, and serve.

MENU

DUMPLINGS AFTER DARK

**Gather round the cabin kitchen table,
flex those folding fingers,
greet, pleat, and eat. Repeat.**

Sriracha-Lime Popcorn   44

**Carrot-Kohlrabi Slaw
with Ginger-Sesame Dressing   75**

**Pork Ginger Scallion
and Shiitake Sake Dumplings   117**

Almond-Tangerine Trifle   154

Fresh-brewed hojicha tea

Bottles of ice-cold Asahi

Yuzu Sours   181

Scotch School

Uncertain how to express your love for the crown jewel of the cabin bar? Mix and match these insider terms to share intriguing tasting notes that will leave no doubt to your knowledge.

"This single malt is a handsome shade of . . ."	"I taste . . ."	"Hmm, that's very . . ."
Straw	Damp wool	Husky
Gold	Fir trees	Peaty
Copper	Moss	Leathery
Corn	Figs	Resinous
Caramel	Fruit cake	Malty
Amber	Marmalade	Marshmallowy
Sherry	Mashed potato	Smoky
Chestnut	Honey	Buttery
Mahogany	Toffee	Chocolaty
Burnt umber	Hay	Nutty
Russet	Tobacco	Fruity
Gingerbread	Shoe polish	Vegetal
Old oak	Burnt toast	Peppery
Loafers	Pipe smoke	Punchy
Taxidermy	Library books	Grandpa-y

One Night in Normandy: Four Calvados Cocktails

Appley, oaky, and altogether appealing, Normandy's famed brandy is famously good for fireside sipping. Warm and fruity, the longer calvados is aged in the barrel, the more woodsy flavors emerge. A young ("fine") calvados will work great in these cocktails, but if you can spring for a VSOP (very superior old pale), which is aged at least four years, by all means, go for the smoother sipper. Each recipe makes one drink.

1. THE BENTLEY

This low-ABV Prohibition-era cocktail, named for a pair of debonair British motorists, is just the cocktail to start your calvados engine.

1½ ounces (45 ml) calvados
1½ ounces (45 ml) Dubonnet Rouge
2 dashes of Peychaud's bitters

Combine the calvados, Dubonnet, and bitters in an ice-filled mixing glass, stir with swagger, and strain into an old-fashioned glass.

2. CIDER SIDECAR

A classic sidecar can be rather bracing with a young brandy, so we've added apple cider to mellow things out.

1 ounce (30 ml) calvados
1 ounce (30 ml) orange liqueur, such as Cointreau
1 ounce (30 ml) fresh lemon juice
1 ounce (30 ml) unfiltered apple juice
Star anise pod
Orange twist

Combine the calvados, orange liqueur, lemon juice, and apple juice in an ice-filled cocktail shaker and shake for 30 seconds until chilled. Strain into a chilled martini glass and garnish with the star anise and orange twist.

3. CALVADOS MILK PUNCH

Give your cocktail a frosty reception by filling the glass with ice cubes while you mix.

1 ounce (30 ml) bourbon
1 ounce (30 ml) calvados
¼ ounce (7 ml) dark rum
½ ounce (15 ml) simple syrup
3½ ounces (105 ml) whole milk
¼ teaspoon pure vanilla extract
Freshly grated nutmeg

Combine the bourbon, calvados, rum, simple syrup, milk, and vanilla in an ice-filled cocktail shaker. Shake for 30 seconds, then strain into a chilled Collins glass filled with ice. Grate nutmeg over the top.

4. CALVADOS HOT TODDY

What separates toddy first-timers from professionals? Prewarming the mug.

3 whole cloves
1 bag chamomile tea, or 1 tablespoon
  loose chamomile tea in an infuser
8 ounces (240 ml) hot water (about
  176°F/80°C)
1 tablespoon honey
1½ ounces (45 ml) calvados
1 teaspoon fresh lemon juice
Strip of green apple peel

Combine the cloves, chamomile tea, and hot water in a mixing glass and let steep for 3 minutes. Meanwhile, warm a mug by filling it with additional hot water. Remove the tea bag, stir in the honey until dissolved, then stir in the calvados and lemon juice. Pour the water out of the mug, carefully place the green apple peel inside, and pour the toddy over the top.

Hot Chocolate Hodgepodge

Please the crowds and warm your mitts with adult- and kid-friendly takes on winter's favorite warmer.

DRINKING CHOCOLATE

MAKES 2

This is a small, sippable, and not-too-sweet hot chocolate for grown-ups. For the most tantalizing texture, make the hot chocolate ahead, cool to room temperature, then refrigerate; reheat before serving.

½ cup (120 ml) milk
½ cup (120 ml) heavy cream
2 ounces (57 g) 70% cacao chocolate, finely chopped
1 ounce (28 g) 85% cacao chocolate, finely chopped
⅛ teaspoon ground cinnamon

Heat the milk and cream in a small saucepan over low heat until very warm (160°F/71C°). Remove from the heat and stir in the chocolate and cinnamon. Let rest for 5 minutes, then whisk again, scraping the sides of the pot with a spatula, until melted and well combined. Return to low heat for 5 minutes to thicken, then serve.

TINY TIP: *For a kicky sippy, add a pinch of cayenne pepper. For a dairy-free drink, substitute ½ cup (120 ml) coconut milk and ½ cup (120 ml) water for the milk and cream.*

SWISS MISTER

MAKES ABOUT 3 CUPS (300 G)

Mix this shelf-stable cocoa mix to have on hand for all the kids crammed into the bunk room, who are looking for instant cozy the second they peel off their snow bibs.

1 cup (70 g) nonfat dry milk powder
¾ cup (95 g) confectioners' sugar
½ cup (50 g) unsweetened Dutch-process cocoa powder
⅓ cup (65 g) granulated sugar
¼ teaspoon kosher salt
Pinch of ground cinnamon

Whisk together the dry milk, confectioners' sugar, cocoa powder, granulated sugar, salt, and cinnamon in a bowl. Store in an airtight container until ready to use. When ready to drink, stir ⅓ cup (33 g) of the mix into an 8-ounce (240 ml) mug full of warm milk. Top with miniature marshmallows or whipped cream.

TINY TIP: *Those taking care of the kids in the bunk room may enjoy a short pour of coffee liqueur in their mugs.*

MINI MARSHMALLOWS

MAKES 1 QUART

Bag these teensy treats as a gift to accompany a jar of cocoa mix.

Nonstick cooking spray
Confectioners' sugar
1 tablespoon unflavored powdered gelatin (from two ¼-ounce/7 g packets)
¾ cup (150 g) granulated sugar
½ cup (120 ml) light corn syrup
⅛ teaspoon kosher salt
1 teaspoon pure vanilla extract
¼ cup (30 g) cornstarch

1. Line two sheet pans with parchment paper, spray with nonstick spray, and use a sifter or fine-mesh strainer to lightly dust the parchment with confectioners' sugar.

2. Pour ¼ cup (60 ml) water into the bowl of a stand mixer fitted with the whisk attachment and sprinkle the gelatin on top. Mix gently with a fork until all the gelatin is incorporated. Let stand until ready for use.

3. Stir together ¼ cup (60 ml) water, the granulated sugar, corn syrup, and salt in a small saucepan. Bring to a boil over medium-high heat, then cook, without stirring, until a candy thermometer reads 240°F (116°C), 5 to 10 minutes.

4. Turn the mixer on low speed and slowly pour in the syrup, avoiding the sides of the bowl and the whisk. Once all the syrup is incorporated, increase the speed to high and mix until the marshmallow mixture is fluffy and glossy and holds a stiff peak, 5 minutes. Stir in the vanilla.

5. Scoop the marshmallow mixture into a piping bag fitted with a ½-inch (1.2 cm) round tip. Pipe about a dozen lines, spaced ½ inch (1.2 cm) apart, down the length of the sheet pan. Repeat with the second pan.

6. Whisk ¼ cup (30 g) confectioners' sugar and the cornstarch together in a small bowl. Sift on top of the marshmallow strips. (Save the remaining dust in an airtight container.) Let the marshmallows set at room temperature for at least 4 hours and up to 12 hours.

7. Roll a pizza wheel or dip a sharp knife into the reserved marshmallow dust and cut the marshmallow strips crosswise into mini marshmallows. Toss the minis in a bowl with more marshmallow dust, taking care to coat the cut sides. Transfer to an airtight container and store at room temperature for up to 2 weeks or in the freezer for up to 3 months.

TINY TIPS: *To make roasting-size marshmallows instead, pour your marshmallow mixture into a loaf pan or square cake pan lined with parchment paper and let set for 8 hours, or preferably overnight. Cut into squares and dust as directed.*

Variety is the spice of life in the cabin; along with the vanilla, spike the mix with 2 teaspoons rum or bourbon, or ½ teaspoon coconut, almond, coffee, or peppermint extract.

Smokey the Pear

MAKES 1

Nearly as likeable as our favorite anti-forest-fire advocate but not as furry (okay, not furry at all), this heady blend of pear brandy and mezcal is best sipped by an outdoor firepit, with a bowl of Five-Spice Candied Cashews (page 43) at hand.

2 ounces (60 ml) pear brandy, such as Clear Creek (see Pantry Provisions, page 218)
¾ ounce (22 ml) mezcal
¾ ounce (22 ml) fresh lemon juice
½ ounce (15 ml) Winter Syrup (recipe follows) or maple syrup
1 (¼-inch-thick/6 mm) lengthwise cross section of pear (see Tiny Tip)

Combine the pear brandy, mezcal, lemon juice, and Winter Syrup in a cocktail shaker. Fill with ice and shake energetically for 30 seconds. Strain into a glass. Float the pear slice on top and serve.

TINY TIP: *For an extra-fancy garnish, carefully slice a pear lengthwise on either side of its stem with a very sharp knife, creating one perfect cross section; eat the rest of the pear, or use it for the Pear-Sultana Chutney on page 63.*

WINTER SYRUP

MAKES ABOUT ½ CUP (120 ML)

½ cup (110 g) light brown sugar
1 cinnamon stick
4 cloves
1 star anise pod

Bring the brown sugar and ½ cup (120 ml) water to a simmer in a small saucepan over medium heat, swirling to dissolve the sugar. Add the spices, reduce the heat to low, and simmer for 5 minutes. Remove from the heat, let steep until completely cool, then remove the spices. Store the syrup in an airtight container in the refrigerator for up to 1 month.

TINY TIP: *Use leftover syrup to spice up hot tea, oatmeal, vanilla bean ice cream, poached pears, pancakes, and roasted root vegetables.*

Oh, What a Nightcap
(a CBD Cocktail)

MAKES 1

Wind down the evening with a calming, sleepy-time sipper that's like a turn-down service for your brain, priming peaceful rest with CBD oil, a deeply relaxing hemp-derived extract that (just to be clear, so you can plan your evening accordingly) does *not* contain THC.

1 ounce (30 ml) gin
1 ounce (30 ml)
   Italicus (see Tiny
   Tips)
¾ ounce (22 ml) fresh
   lemon juice
¾ ounce (22 ml)
   Lavender Simple
   Syrup (recipe follows)
1 teaspoon orgeat
   (see Tiny Tips)
1 egg white
CBD oil
Soda water, to fill
   (about 2 ounces/
   60 ml)
Lavender sprig

Combine the gin, Italicus, lemon juice, lavender simple syrup, orgeat, and egg white in a cocktail shaker. Shake it like you mean it for 30 seconds. Add a handful of ice and shake for 30 more seconds. Drop 10 mg of CBD into an 8-ounce (240 ml) glass. Strain the cocktail into the glass. Top with soda water, garnish with the lavender sprig, and call it a night.

TINY TIPS: *Italicus, a bergamot-based aperitif, is a beautiful bottle on any bar, and makes an A+ spritz, too, but if you do not wish to purchase it, ½ ounce (15 ml) St-Germain elderflower liqueur and ½ ounce (15 ml) more gin is a welcome substitution.*

Look for orgeat in the liquor store near the bitters; save the rest for mai tais.

LAVENDER SIMPLE SYRUP

MAKES ABOUT ½ CUP (120 ML)

½ cup (100 g) sugar
½ cup (120 ml) water
1 teaspoon dried
   lavender buds

Bring the sugar and water to a gentle simmer in a small pot. Cook, stirring frequently, until the sugar has dissolved and the syrup is clear. Remove from the heat and add the lavender. Let steep for 20 minutes. Strain the syrup into a squeeze bottle or lidded jar and refrigerate for up to 1 month.

CHAPTER 7

Morning Meal

When facing a full day of forging through snowy forests on snowshoes, breaking new cross-country ski trails, mastering the triple lutz on the village ice rink, and taking top honors at the local bonspiel (aka curling tournament), you'd best start with an equally bold breakfast: bowls brimming with steel-cut oats and all the toppings, stacks of warm-spiced Pumpkin-Ginger Waffles with Cider Syrup, and cast-iron skillets piled with Red Flannel Hash and spicy Chilly-quiles Rojos. Add a few cups of strong coffee and a round of equally brawny Hail(storm) Caesars (page 168), and you're ready to take on anything, even if it's just a day of rigorous fireside lounging with a good book (you can't go wrong revisiting C. S. Lewis's classically wintry *The Lion, the Witch and the Wardrobe,* but if your cabin's particularly isolated, maybe save *The Winter People* for when you get home).

Mountaintop Muesli

SERVES 4

Swiss physician Maximilian Bircher-Benner's prescription for a healthy breakfast of soaked oats, fruit, and nuts has kept skiers' and dogsled racers' tummies from grumbling during physically exerting days since 1900. Our favorite iteration of these OG overnight oats calls for a grated apple stirred in for sweetness and a healthy pinch of ginger for health. Wait to add crunchy almonds and coconut flakes just before serving—"Mush!" should be the cue to get sled dogs moving, not an accurate descriptor of your breakfast.

2 cups (180 g) rolled oats
2 cups (480 ml) oat milk, or preferred milk
1 Honeycrisp apple, grated
2 teaspoons ground cinnamon
¼ teaspoon ground ginger
1½ cups (360 ml) whole-milk yogurt
2 tablespoons honey, plus more for drizzling
½ cup (50 g) sliced almonds
¼ cup (35 g) dried cherries
¼ cup (20 g) unsweetened shredded coconut

1. Toast the oats in a 12-inch dry skillet over medium heat until fragrant, about 3 minutes. Transfer to a medium bowl and stir in the oat milk, grated apple, cinnamon, and ginger. Soak for at least 30 minutes or ideally overnight.

2. Whisk together the yogurt and honey in a small bowl. Cover and refrigerate. Combine the almonds, cherries, and coconut in a small container and set aside at room temperature.

3. When ready to serve, divide the soaked oats among four bowls and sprinkle half the almonds, cherries, and coconut flakes on top. Divide the honey yogurt between the bowls, then sprinkle with the remaining topping. Drizzle with honey and serve.

The Ultimate Oatmeal Bar

MAKES 3 CUPS (720 ML)

Time, love, and tenderness are all it takes to make an early '90s Michael Bolton smash hit. But also, the perfect bowl of oatmeal. That's because the best bowl is filled with steel-cut oats (oat groats sliced with a steel blade), which take a bit longer to cook than rolled oats (which are pressed) and instant oats (which are not great). If you don't have a half hour for breakfast prep in the morning, you can make a big batch of oatmeal at the beginning of the week and warm portions all the mornings that follow. Or you could use those 30 minutes to set up the end-all oatmeal bar and thereby secure your spot as breakfast MVP.

1½ cups (360 ml) milk
½ teaspoon kosher salt
1 cup (155 g) steel-cut oats

Combine the milk, salt and 1½ cups (360 ml) water in a saucepan and bring to a boil. Add the oats and stir. Reduce the heat to low and simmer for 30 minutes, stirring occasionally. Let cool for 5 minutes before serving.

Orange Whiskey Butter (see page 90) + pecans + cream

Five-Spice Candied Cashews (page 43) + chopped dried apricots + cream

Starfruit + pomegranate arils + kiwi + honey

Raspberries + pistachios + Nutella

Apples + almonds + maple syrup

Chopped dates + pears + hazelnuts

MENU

BLACKCOMB BRUNCH

**Peak views optional;
peak appetite mandatory.**

Mountaintop Muesli   192

**Winter Citrus Salad
with Honey Citronette   195**

**Pecan Popovers
with Spiced Apple Butter   202**

Red Flannel Hash with Eggs   208

Coffee, and lots of it

Hail(storm) Caesars   168

Winter Citrus Salad with Honey Citronette

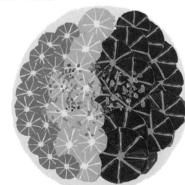

SERVES 4

If you're sorely missing that great orange orb in the sky right around mid-January, use the smaller, less molten ones at the market to brighten things up. We love the sweet simplicity of this honey-citrus dressing, but if you're in a hurry, just drizzle the salad with olive oil, squeeze a lime over the top, sprinkle it with flaky sea salt, and call it a (long, dark) day.

HONEY CITRONETTE

1 teaspoon grated lime zest
2 tablespoons fresh lime juice
1 tablespoon honey
Pinch of kosher salt
3 tablespoons extra-virgin olive oil

SALAD

2 large Ruby Red grapefruits
2 large Cara Cara or regular navel oranges
2 blood oranges
3 tangerines
¼ cup (13 g) fresh mint leaves
2 tablespoons coarsely chopped shelled roasted salted pistachios
Flaky sea salt

AT THE CABIN

• Microplane grater

1. To make the citronette: Whisk together the lime zest, lime juice, honey, and salt in a small bowl, then whisk in the olive oil.

2. To make the salad: Place a cutting board inside a rimmed sheet pan (this will keep citrus juice from dripping everywhere). Carefully trim the peel and pith from the grapefruits, oranges, and tangerines with a very sharp knife (we like using a thin, flexible serrated tomato knife), then slice each fruit crosswise into ¼-inch-thick (6 mm) wheels. Artfully arrange the citrus on a serving platter. (The citrus can be refrigerated for up to 2 hours before serving.)

3. Just before serving, drizzle the citronette over the sliced citrus. Coarsely chop the mint leaves, and sprinkle them over the top. Sprinkle with the pistachios and a generous pinch of flaky salt, and serve.

TINY TIP: *All this gorgeous citrus means a whole lot of zest—use your Microplane grater to remove all of it before trimming and slicing the fruit, then mix it into Orange–Earl Grey Cream Scones (page 216), Tangerine Dream Curd (page 153), or Orange Whiskey Butter (see page 90); or freeze it for up to 1 month.*

Lemon–Vanilla Bean Aebleskiver

MAKES ABOUT 28

Aebleskiver—pillowy little Scandinavian pancake balls baked in a specially designed cast-iron pan—means "apple slices" in Danish, because tradition calls for tucking a wee slice of apple into the center of each pancake. While we forgo the apple in favor of vanilla bean and fresh lemon zest, these are nothing short (and round) of delicious. If you're tempted to whisk the eggs in whole versus whipping the egg whites separately, you can, but the pancakes won't be quite as fluffy, and may take a bit longer to fully cook through. For sourcing the proper pan, turning tips, and garnish guidance, see Be an Aebleskiver Overachiever on page 198.

2 cups (250 g) all-purpose flour
3 tablespoons sugar
2 teaspoons grated lemon zest
2 teaspoons baking powder
½ teaspoon baking soda
½ teaspoon kosher salt
2 cups (480 ml) buttermilk
2 large eggs, separated
2 tablespoons unsalted butter, melted and slightly cooled, plus more for brushing
2 teaspoons pure vanilla extract
1 vanilla bean, split lengthwise and seeds scraped out
Toppings (see page 199)

AT THE CABIN

- Aebleskiver pan
- Wooden skewer

1. Whisk together the flour, sugar, lemon zest, baking powder, baking soda, and salt in a large bowl. Whisk together the buttermilk, egg yolks, melted butter, vanilla extract, and vanilla seeds in a medium bowl until smooth. Pour the wet ingredients into the dry ingredients and whisk until smooth.

2. Beat the egg whites in a small bowl with a handheld mixer until they hold stiff peaks. Using a spatula, carefully fold the egg whites into the batter until just combined.

3. Heat an aebleskiver pan over medium or medium-low heat (don't let the pan get too hot) and generously brush each hollow with melted butter. Completely fill each well with batter (use a cookie scoop to help mitigate mess). The aebleskiver edges will begin to bubble, and they will begin to form a golden crust; this takes anywhere from 15 seconds to 1 minute, depending on how hot your pan is (but remember, don't let your pan get too hot!).

4. Use a wooden skewer to gently rotate each pancake a quarter turn to the left, letting the batter flow down into the well and bake. Wait 10 to 15 seconds, then rotate each pancake a quarter turn north, then south, each time letting the batter flow down into the well and bake. Keep rotating the pancakes back and forth and to the left, slowly releasing all the batter and gently shaping them into balls.

5. When each pancake is left with just a small hole on the right side, use the skewer to gently lift, turn, tuck, and shape each pancake into a closed ball. Let the balls cook for several minutes, rotating them often to prevent burning, until they're cooked through and dark gold, 5 to 7 minutes (pull a test pancake from the pan and break it in half to be sure).

6. Serve the aebleskiver with a variety of delicious dips and toppings, plus hot chocolate (see page 186) at breakfast, or glogg (see page 175) for a post-sled-run afternoon fika.

Be an Aebleskiver Overachiever

Yes, you can serve these delightful little Scandinavian pancake balls with jam and be done, or you can reach for the aebleskiver stars—experimenting with creative mix-ins, offering multiple dipping sauces, and honing your turning technique to achieve perfectly round orbs. Here are your aebleskiver-baking basics, with a cherry (compote) on top.

Plan Your Pan

This is one recipe that really does need special equipment—an aebleskiver pan (see Pantry Provisions, page 218). Find a basic version at your favorite kitchen shop or online for around $25; nonstick is more forgiving for beginners, while cast iron is traditional and timeless. For a vintage version that's already been broken in, check eBay or Etsy. Most pans make seven aebleskiver at a time, so consider investing in two if you've got a big breakfast crew.

Beat the Heat

Don't let your pan overheat, or you'll end up with burnt balls and gummy, underdone centers. Keep the heat steady, even, and medium to medium-low; between batches, use a silicone pastry brush to coat each divot with plenty of butter to prevent sticking.

Fill 'Er Up

If you want picture-perfect aebleskiver—gorgeous, plump golden spheres even a normally stoic Scandinavian would get emotional about—fill each well right to the top, nearly to overflowing, and add a little more batter to the pan after the first turn. If you're Team

Oblong, and aren't as concerned about aesthetics, take the relaxing route and fill the pan's divots three-quarters of the way. Because the fact is, even if your aebleskiver turn out lumpy or lopsided, they're just as delicious.

Stuff It

Think the only thing better than a hot freshly baked aebleskiver is a hot freshly baked aebleskiver with a Nutella center? You are not wrong. To stuff your 'skivers, fill each of the pan's divots about halfway with batter, add fun fillings (apple slices, applesauce, mashed banana, fruit jam, bacon jam, tart cherries, fresh berries, chocolate chips, chopped nuts, nut butter, cookie butter, Nutella, etc.), cover with enough batter to fill the rest of the divot, and proceed.

All in the Wrist

If you've ever watched a Japanese street food vendor turn takoyaki at what looks like the speed of light, you know the drill—pay close attention to your aebleskiver, turning them often to bake evenly and avoid burning. Turn and tuck the pancakes as directed on pages 196–197, using a wooden skewer, toothpick, chopstick, or, if you're being extra authentic, a knitting needle.

The Pan That Can

Take your new aebleskiver pan international, without leaving the kitchen—use it to try your hand at Japan's famed octopus-stuffed takoyaki, Dutch poffertjes (similar to aebleskiver but made with yeast), India's savory rice-and-lentil-based paddu, or Thailand's khanom khrok, a sweet street food staple made with rice flour and coconut milk. And if you packed the pan but forgot a skillet, use it to fry eggs, albeit rather clumsily.

You Flip, I Flip, We Dip

Your aebleskiver are done, but the fun's just beginning. Gild them with the following garnishes, and offer up a variety of these delicious dips (all of which are interchangeable).

TOP WITH	DIP IN
Confectioners' sugar	Cinnamon applesauce
Cinnamon sugar	Strawberry or raspberry jam
Cardamom sugar	Nutella
Pure maple syrup	Melted chocolate
Bacon bits	Vanilla bean whipped cream
Amarena cherry syrup	Cider Syrup (see page 205)
Fresh berries	Brown butter
Whipped cream	Cherry or berry compote
Grated citrus zest	Tangerine Dream Curd (page 153)

Corn Cakes with Brown Sugar–Blueberry Compote

MAKES 20 (3-INCH/8 CM) PANCAKES

Besides long underwear and wool socks, there's no better base layer for a day in the snow than a stack of these golden corn cakes topped with warm blueberries. A stone-ground cornmeal with a little heft (we like Bob's Red Mill) lends the best texture for these flapjacks, and if you're of the opinion that no wintertime pancake breakfast is complete without breakfast sausages or bacon, by all means, go for it.

BLUEBERRY COMPOTE

2 (12-ounce/340 g) bags frozen blueberries
⅔ cup packed (150 g) light brown sugar
2 teaspoons fresh lemon juice

PANCAKES

1 cup (180 g) fine yellow cornmeal
4 tablespoons (½ stick/60 g) unsalted butter, melted and cooled
2 large eggs
1½ cups (360 ml) whole milk
1½ cups (190 g) all-purpose flour
2 tablespoons sugar
1 teaspoon baking powder
1 teaspoon kosher salt
Neutral oil, such as safflower or grapeseed, for greasing

1. To make the compote: Stir together ⅔ cup (160 ml) water, the blueberries, and the brown sugar in a large saucepan. Bring to a boil, then reduce the heat to maintain a simmer and cook, stirring often, for 15 to 20 minutes, until the berries begin to burst. Remove from the heat, stir in the lemon juice, and let cool for 5 minutes before serving.

2. To make the pancakes: Measure the cornmeal into a large bowl and stir in 1 cup (240 ml) boiling water. Let cool for 5 minutes, then stir in the butter. Whisk together the eggs and the milk in a medium bowl, then stir the egg mixture into the cornmeal mixture. Add the flour, sugar, baking powder, and salt. Stir until just incorporated.

3. Heat a 12-inch (30 cm) cast-iron skillet over medium heat. Brush with oil. Working in batches, use a pancake pen or spouted ladle to pour ¼ cup (60 ml) of batter into the skillet and cook until bubbles form on the surface and pop, about 2 minutes. Flip and cook for an additional 2 minutes until golden brown with crisp edges. Stack on a plate and repeat with the remaining batter, brushing the pan with more oil as needed. Serve with the compote alongside.

TINY TIPS: *For no-fuss bacon-makin', place the strips on a sheet pan in a single layer and bake in a preheated 425°F (220°C) oven for 15 minutes, or until crisp. Flip once. Transfer to a plate lined with paper towels.*

The blueberry compote recipe yields plenty, since no one likes to run out; stir any leftovers into yogurt and top with granola.

End on a Good Note

Much of this book is devoted to the particularities of planning and hosting a cozy cabin holiday, but we're also quite delighted to be on the receiving end of the fuss. When you're lucky enough to be that thunderstruck-with-gratitude guest, your top priority is to make sure that happens again, as often as possible—say, same time next year? The best way to set the stage for your triumphant return is with a charming thank-you note and, if you want to put a cherry on top, a thoughtful gift. Send both immediately or else risk your inspired moment of civility falling to the wayside faster than your New Year's resolution to floss. If the perfect treat has already sprung to mind, hurray! If you're drawing a blank, might we suggest the following?

1. Custom portrait of the cabin (paperfinger.com) **2.** View-Master with a reel of vacation photos (image3D.com) **3.** Snow-shoveling IOU **4.** A bottle of Boozy Orange Bourbon Eggnog (page 174) **5.** *Charade* (The Criterion Collection) **6.** Covetable mugs (tannergoods.com) **7.** The mittens you were knitting by the fire **8.** Small Fry skillet (greatjones.com)

Pecan Popovers
with Spiced Apple Butter

MAKES 6 POPOVERS

When it comes to food mills—the utmost old-fashioned kitchen gadget—a vintage Foley is still the best. If you don't spy one at that estate sale you passed on the way to the cabin, peel the apples before cooking, then transfer to a blender to purée. If you find yourself without a popover pan, see the Tiny Tips on page 86 for a muffin-tin alternative.

1 cup (125 g)
   all-purpose flour
2 tablespoons sugar
1 teaspoon ground
   cinnamon
½ teaspoon kosher salt
Pinch of freshly grated
   nutmeg
2 large eggs
1 cup (240 ml) milk
¼ cup (30 g) finely
   chopped pecans
6 teaspoons neutral
   oil, such as safflower
   or grapeseed
Spiced Apple Butter
   (recipe follows),
   for serving

AT THE CABIN
- **Popover pan**

1. Set a popover pan on a sheet pan on the lowest rack of the oven. Move the other racks to the top positions and preheat the oven to 450°F (230°C).

2. Whisk together the flour, sugar, cinnamon, salt, and nutmeg in a medium bowl. In a separate bowl, whisk the eggs and milk for 1 minute, until frothy. Gradually whisk the dry ingredients into the wet ingredients until smooth. Stir in the pecans, then transfer to a spouted container. (The batter can be covered and refrigerated overnight; set it on the counter for at least 30 minutes to bring it to room temperature before baking.)

3. Remove the sheet pan with the popover pan from the oven and set it on a heat-safe surface. Measure 1 teaspoon of the oil into each well. Divide the batter evenly among the wells. Return the pan to the oven. Bake for 20 minutes, then reduce the oven temperature to 350°F (180°C) and bake for 10 minutes more until the popovers are puffed and golden, with crisp tops. (Resist the urge to open the oven and peek during baking! You could deflate the popovers and, in doing so, your ego.) Remove from the oven and invert the pan to remove the popovers. Serve immediately, with a generous slathering of apple butter.

SPICED APPLE BUTTER

MAKES 2 CUPS (480 ML)

4 pounds (1.8 kg) sweet-tart red apples such as Fuji, Gala, or Pink Lady (about 8), cored and cut into chunks
2 cups (480 ml) unfiltered apple juice (sometimes sold as cider)
2 star anise pods
1 cinnamon stick
2 tablespoons fresh lemon juice
½ cup (100 g) granulated sugar
½ cup packed (110 g) brown sugar
1 teaspoon pure vanilla extract

AT THE CABIN
• Food mill
• Immersion blender

1. Position a rack in the center of the oven and preheat the oven to 300°F (150°C).

2. Combine the apples, apple juice, star anise, and cinnamon stick in a large (at least 4-quart/4 L) Dutch oven. Bring to a boil, then reduce the heat to maintain a simmer and cook until the apples are soft but still holding their shape, about 20 minutes. Remove and discard the spices.

3. Working in batches, pass the apples and liquid through a food mill set over a bowl. Discard the skin and seeds. Add the lemon juice, granulated sugar, brown sugar, and vanilla to the puréed apples. Return the mixture to the Dutch oven.

4. Bake, uncovered, for 2½ hours, stirring every 30 minutes, until the apple butter has reduced to a jammy consistency and is glossy and deep caramel in color. Enjoy the rustic texture as it is, or whiz with an immersion blender until smooth. Transfer the apple butter to a pint (480 ml) jar, cover with the lid, and let cool on the counter for at least 2 hours. Store in the refrigerator for up to 3 weeks. Serve with popovers, crumpets, or English muffins, or on a cheese board with crackers.

TINY TIP: *If there's a Dutch oven scarcity at the cabin, cook the apples on the stovetop in a large saucepan, then transfer the purée to a casserole dish to bake.*

Pumpkin-Ginger Waffles with Cider Syrup

SERVES 4

While you can certainly drown these fresh-ginger-spiced pumpkin waffles in maple syrup, we like mixing things up a bit with a deep, dark, richly reduced homemade apple cider syrup. For a quick no-mess morning meal before heading to the sno-park, cook and separate waffles into sections, freeze them flat on a sheet pan, store in a resealable bag in the freezer, then pop into the toaster for a few minutes before serving.

6 tablespoons
(¾ stick/85 g)
unsalted butter
2 cups (250 g)
all-purpose flour
1 tablespoon ground
cinnamon
2 teaspoons baking
powder
1 teaspoon baking soda
1 teaspoon ground
allspice
1 teaspoon freshly
grated nutmeg
¾ teaspoon kosher salt
½ teaspoon ground
cloves
1½ cups (360 ml)
buttermilk
⅔ cup (160 ml) canned
pure pumpkin purée
2 large eggs
¼ cup (60 ml) pure
maple syrup
1 tablespoon grated
fresh ginger
2 teaspoons pure
vanilla extract
Cider Syrup (recipe
follows), for serving

1. Preheat a waffle iron to your desired setting (we like medium to medium-high, for crispness' sake). Melt the butter in a small saucepan and set aside to cool slightly.

2. Whisk together the flour, cinnamon, baking powder, baking soda, allspice, nutmeg, salt, and cloves in a large bowl. Whisk together the buttermilk, pumpkin, eggs, maple syrup, ginger, vanilla, and melted butter in a medium bowl until smooth. Pour the wet ingredients into the dry ingredients and stir until just combined (the batter will be thick).

3. Spoon the batter into the waffle iron and cook the waffles until you reach the desired crispness. Serve with cider syrup and a stick of room-temperature butter (much easier to spread).

TINY TIPS: *For extra credit, sprinkle the buttery, cidery waffles with maple pecans (see page 76).*

If baking for a full table, make all the waffles at once, laying them out on a wire rack as you go (so they don't get soggy bottoms from sitting on a plate). When finished, place the entire batch directly on the oven rack at 350°F (180°C) until re-crisped, 3 to 5 minutes.

AT THE CABIN
• Waffle iron

CIDER SYRUP

MAKES ABOUT 1 CUP (240 ML)

Since this syrup doesn't need much minding, you can have it simmering in the background while you make coffee and wrangle waffle ingredients. If you have any left over post-wafflefest, pour it over pancakes, oatmeal, baked apples and pears, or vanilla bean ice cream, or add a few tablespoons to apple pie (or strudel; see page 158) filling for extra-concentrated flavor.

4 cups (1 L) unfiltered apple cider
1 cinnamon stick
¼ cup packed (55 g) light brown sugar
2 tablespoons unsalted butter
1 tablespoon fresh lemon juice
Pinch of kosher salt

1. Stir together the apple cider, cinnamon stick, brown sugar, butter, lemon juice, and salt in a 3-quart (3 L) saucepan. Bring to a boil over medium-high heat, then boil the syrup, reducing the heat if necessary so it doesn't burn or bubble over, until it's dark, glossy, and reduced to 1 cup (240 ml), about 25 minutes.

2. Let cool slightly, then remove the cinnamon stick and strain through a fine-mesh sieve to remove any froth. If not using immediately, transfer to an 8-ounce (240 ml) mason jar and cool to room temperature, stirring occasionally. Store in the refrigerator for up to 2 weeks; rewarm in a small saucepan over medium-low heat before serving.

Build a Better Snowperson Pancake

Forget the corncob pipe and the button nose and lay out a bonanza of edible adornments for your breakfast bunch.

Frosty Morning French Toast: Six Tasty Twists

Does it seem impossible to improve on the perfection that is French toast—thick slices of warm, golden, custard-soaked challah piled high and drowned in melted butter and pure maple syrup? Yes, yes, 4,804 times yes (which is, coincidentally, how many meters Mont Blanc hits on the French Alps height chart). But if you're looking for a tempting twist on your everyday toppers, here are six highly appetizing alternatives.

1. Caramelized bananas + salted honey butter + rum raisins + freshly grated nutmeg + toasted walnuts

2. Roasted pears + brown sugar whipped cream + pinch of ground cardamom + toasted pecans

3. Sautéed spiced apples + Cider Syrup (see page 205) + cinnamon crème fraîche + sprinkle of ground cinnamon

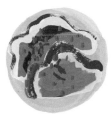

4. Raspberry jam + pistachio butter + melted dark chocolate + roasted salted pistachios + grated chocolate

5. Caramelized pineapple + Dark Rum Sauce (see page 160) + toasted shredded coconut + fresh mint

6. Tangerine Dream Curd (page 153) + orange slices + Cointreau caramel (see page 154) + grated orange zest

Red Flannel Hash with Eggs

SERVES 2 TO 4

Feed your inner lumberjack and Babe the Blue Ox, too, with this hearty breakfast, a vibrant medley of winter root vegetables tossed together in a single skillet. Nestle four eggs directly into the hash for quick, one-pan cleanup or, if serving more than two hungry people, avoid overcrowding the skillet by frying two eggs per person in olive oil in a separate pan.

2 golden beets, peeled and cut into ½-inch (1.2 cm) dice

1 pound (455 g) sweet potatoes, cut into ½-inch (1.2 cm) dice

¼ cup (60 ml) sour cream

1 tablespoon prepared horseradish

1½ teaspoons fresh lemon juice

Extra-virgin olive oil

1 cup (195 g) chopped corned beef (see Tiny Tips)

½ medium onion, diced

2 tablespoons unsalted butter

1 teaspoon kosher salt

½ teaspoon freshly ground black pepper

2 cups packed (130 g) thinly sliced stemmed kale leaves

4 large eggs

½ cup (35 g) coarsely chopped fresh soft herbs (dill, mint, chives, or a combo), for garnish

1. Set a steamer basket in a large pot filled with a few inches (5 to 7.5 cm) of water and bring the water to a simmer over high heat; reduce the heat to maintain a simmer. Place the beets in the steamer, cover, and steam for 2 minutes, then carefully add the sweet potatoes to the basket, cover, and steam the vegetables for 3 minutes more, until fork-tender. Remove from the heat.

2. Meanwhile, whisk together the sour cream, horseradish, and lemon juice in a small bowl. Set aside.

3. Warm 1 tablespoon olive oil in a large skillet over medium-high heat. Add the corned beef and cook until crisp. Transfer to a plate with a slotted spoon. Reduce the heat to medium, add the onion to the rendered fat in the pan, and cook for 3 minutes, or until the onion begins to become translucent but is not yet cooked through. Add 1 tablespoon olive oil and the butter to the skillet, then add the sweet potatoes and beets and toss to coat. Season with the salt and pepper. Cook, undisturbed, for 5 minutes, until the potatoes begin to crisp, then add the kale and cook until wilted, about 2 minutes. Return the corned beef to the pan and cook for 3 minutes, or until the corned beef is heated through and the vegetables are tender but still holding their shape.

4. Make four deep indentations in the hash with the back of a spoon and crack an egg into each one. Add ½ teaspoon water to the inside of the skillet's lid (or swiftly run the lid through the faucet) and cover the skillet to quickly steam the eggs. Cook until the egg whites are set but the yolk is still runny, about 3 minutes.

5. Divide the hash and eggs among plates and top each serving with a dollop of the horseradish cream and a sprinkle of herbs.

TINY TIPS: *Chop the beets and sweets the night before to cut down on prep time in the morning.*

If you're not making the most of Saint Patrick's Day leftovers, ask the deli counterperson for 4 ounces (115 g) corned beef, sliced ¼ inch (6 mm) thick, or substitute bacon or leftover sausages or ham.

Chilly-quiles Rojos

SERVES 4

See the Tiny Tip for instructions on how to make your own corn tortilla chips, but if you're in a hurry to get out into the flurry, just use a (very) sturdy store-bought chip—we like Have'a corn chips; they're thick and crispy and won't go completely soggy on you the second they're tossed with the sauce. For a spicy, satisfying lodge lunch, top your chilaquiles with fried eggs and serve them with warmed black beans or pinto beans.

SAUCE

- 1 (14.5-ounce/411 g) can fire-roasted diced tomatoes, with their juices
- ⅓ cup (60 g) coarsely chopped white onion
- 3 (about 2-inch/5 cm) canned chipotle peppers in adobo sauce, plus (optional) 1 tablespoon adobo sauce
- 1 jalapeño pepper, coarsely chopped
- 2 large garlic cloves
- 1 teaspoon kosher salt, plus more as needed
- ¼ teaspoon freshly ground black pepper, plus more as needed

1. To make the sauce: Combine the tomatoes, onion, chipotle peppers, adobo sauce, jalapeño, garlic, salt, and pepper in the bowl of a high-speed blender. Add ⅓ cup (80 ml) water, and puree until very smooth.

2. Transfer the sauce to a large skillet and simmer over medium heat until slightly darker and thicker, about 5 minutes. (You may need to cover the skillet if the sauce is trying to splash onto the cabin ceiling.) Taste and season with more salt, pepper, and adobo sauce if desired, then remove from the heat.

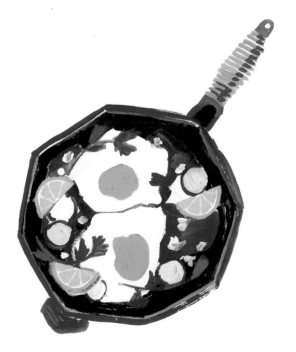

CHILAQUILES

8 large eggs (optional)

6 ounces (170 g) sturdy corn tortilla chips (about 6 cups)

¼ cup (60 ml) Mexican crema (or sour cream, thinned with a splash of milk)

1 avocado, pitted, halved, and sliced

½ onion, sliced or diced (optional)

2 ounces (57 g) queso fresco or Cotija cheese, crumbled

2 radishes, thinly sliced

¼ cup (13 g) fresh cilantro leaves

1 lime, cut into 8 wedges

3. To make the chilaquiles: If you're making eggs, fry or scramble them in a separate skillet. Add the tortilla chips to the skillet with the sauce, and gently toss until completely coated. Arrange the chilaquiles in an even layer in the skillet and drizzle with the crema or sour cream. Top with the eggs (if using) and avocado. If you love fresh onion on chilaquiles, sprinkle some over the top. Sprinkle with the cheese, radishes, and cilantro, and garnish with the lime wedges. Serve immediately—chilly-quiles are delightful, but super-soggy-quiles aren't quite as much, so plan on cleaning your plate (well, skillet) in one sitting.

TINY TIP: *To fry your own corn tortillas, cut 8 corn tortillas into 6 wedges each. Heat 1 inch (2.5 cm) of vegetable or grapeseed oil in a large skillet over medium-high heat until shimmering (350°F/180°C). Fry the tortilla wedges in a single layer (it'll take a few batches), turning them a couple of times and gently pressing down on them with tongs so they stay submerged, until golden brown, about 2 minutes. Remove with a slotted spoon and drain on paper towels. Let cool completely before using for the chilaquiles or serving.*

Buckwheat, Black Pepper, and Thyme Biscuits with Sherry Shiitake Gravy

SERVES 4

If you can't find shiitake mushrooms, try cremini, oyster, portobello, and/or chanterelle. This is an easy make-ahead brunch; the biscuits can be prepped and frozen until ready to bake, while the gravy will keep for about two days in the refrigerator. If you prefer a smoother gravy, take all or part of it for a spin in the blender, then return it to the pan and reheat it before serving.

BISCUITS

1½ cups (190 g) all-purpose flour, plus more for dusting

½ cup (60 g) buckwheat flour

2 teaspoons baking powder

1½ teaspoons minced fresh thyme

1 teaspoon kosher salt

1 teaspoon freshly ground black pepper

½ teaspoon baking soda

½ cup (1 stick/115g) cold unsalted butter, cut into cubes

¾ cup (180 ml) buttermilk, plus more for brushing

1. To make the biscuits: Line a rimmed half sheet pan with parchment paper.

2. Whisk together the all-purpose flour, buckwheat flour, baking powder, thyme, salt, pepper, and baking soda in a large bowl. Add the butter and work it into the flour mixture with your hands (pretend you're snapping your fingers together) until coarse crumbs form. Add the buttermilk and work it in with your hands or a fork until a shaggy dough forms. (Work as fast as you can; the less you handle the dough, the flakier the biscuits will be.)

3. Turn the dough out onto a lightly floured surface and fold it over itself five times to help bring the dough together and create layers. Pat the dough into a 1-inch-thick (2.5 cm) rectangle. Use a pastry scraper to cut it crosswise into four equal sections, then cut each section in half to make eight square biscuits total. Place the biscuits on the prepared sheet pan, giving them room to spread, and chill them in the refrigerator while the oven preheats, about 15 minutes. (Or, freeze them until solid, put them in an airtight container, and freeze to have on hand the moment a biscuit craving strikes; just add a few minutes to the baking time.)

4. Preheat the oven to 425°F (220°C).

GRAVY

- 2 tablespoons unsalted butter
- 2 large shallots, minced (about ½ cup/85 g)
- 3 large garlic cloves, minced (about 1 tablespoon)
- ½ pound (225 g) shiitake mushrooms, stemmed and thinly sliced
- 2 teaspoons minced fresh thyme
- ½ teaspoon kosher salt
- ¼ cup (30 g) all-purpose flour
- ½ cup (120 ml) dry sherry
- 2 cups (480 ml) chicken stock
- 2 tablespoons heavy cream
- Freshly ground black pepper

- ¼ cup (13 g) coarsely chopped fresh flat-leaf parsley, for garnish

AT THE CABIN
- Blender (optional)

5. Brush the tops of the biscuits with buttermilk and bake until golden brown, 15 to 18 minutes. Remove the biscuits from the oven and let cool on the sheet pan for 5 minutes. (Although far better fresh, the biscuits will keep in an airtight container at room temperature for up to 3 days; wrap them in aluminum foil and rewarm in a preheated 350°F/180°C oven for 10 minutes before serving.)

6. In the meantime, make the gravy: Melt the butter in a large skillet over medium-high heat. Add the shallot and garlic and cook until fragrant, about 30 seconds. Add the mushrooms, thyme, and salt and cook until the mushrooms are tender, 5 to 7 minutes. Add the flour and stir until it has been absorbed, about 30 seconds. Stir in the sherry, then the stock, reduce the heat, and let the gravy simmer until thick, 5 to 7 minutes. Remove from the heat, stir in the cream, and season with salt and pepper. (The gravy can be stored in an airtight container in the refrigerator for up to 2 days; reheat in a large saucepan over medium-low heat before serving.)

7. Split the biscuits in half horizontally and place two biscuit bottoms on each of four plates. Divide the gravy among the plates, spooning it over the biscuits. Prop the biscuit tops on top, sprinkle with the parsley, and serve immediately.

Swedish Cardamom Rolls

MAKES 12

For the easiest morning kitchen machinations, prep and refrigerate these rolls the night before. In the morning, let them rise in a warm spot while you revive the fire and task the troops with finding their ice hockey sticks.

DOUGH

4 tablespoons (½ stick/60 g) unsalted butter, plus more for greasing
2½ cups (315 g) all-purpose flour, plus more for dusting
3 tablespoons sugar
1 tablespoon cardamom seeds, ground (see Tiny Tips)
1 teaspoon kosher salt
1 (¼-ounce/7 g) packet active dry yeast (2¼ teaspoons)
¼ cup (60 ml) warm water (110° to 115°F/ 43° to 46°C)
½ cup (120 ml) whole milk
1 large egg, beaten

FILLING

2 tablespoons unsalted butter
¼ cup packed (55 g) light brown sugar
¼ cup (50 g) granulated sugar
1 tablespoon cardamom seeds, ground (see Tiny Tips)

TOPPING

1 egg, beaten with 1 tablespoon milk, for egg wash
2 teaspoons sugar (see Tiny Tips)

1. To make the dough: Butter a large bowl and set it aside. Stir together the flour, sugar, cardamom, and salt in a large bowl. Combine the yeast and warm water in a small bowl and let sit until foamy, about 5 minutes.

2. Melt the 4 tablespoons butter in a small saucepan over low heat, then remove from the heat and stir in the milk (the mixture should be lukewarm; if it's too hot, let it cool a bit, or it may kill the yeast).

3. Add the egg, yeast mixture, and milk-butter mixture to the dry ingredients, and mix until a shaggy, sticky dough forms.

4. Turn the dough out onto a lightly floured surface and knead it by hand, sprinkling with additional flour as needed, until smooth and shiny, about 5 minutes. Transfer the dough to the greased bowl, cover with a kitchen towel, and let rise in a warm place until puffy and nearly doubled in size, 1½ to 2 hours.

5. While the dough is rising, make the filling: Melt the butter in a small saucepan over low heat, then remove from the heat. Mix together the brown sugar, granulated sugar, and cardamom in a small bowl, breaking up any brown sugar lumps with your fingers.

6. Line a rimmed half sheet pan with parchment paper. Transfer the dough to a lightly floured surface and roll it into a 12-by-21-inch (30 by 53 cm) rectangle. Brush the melted butter over the dough, then sprinkle the cardamom-sugar mixture evenly over the top. Fold the dough in thirds, like a letter, then rotate it a quarter turn so the ends are on your left and right and lightly roll it out into a 12-by-8-inch (30 by 20 cm) rectangle.

7. Cut the dough into twelve 1-by-8-inch (2.5 by 20 cm) strips with a pizza slicer (or a very sharp knife). Pick up one strip and lightly stretch it to elongate it, then twist the strip around your thumb, index finger, and middle finger to create a knotlike bun. (Separate your fingers slightly as you twist to create space to poke the ends through.) Tuck the ends in securely and set the bun on the prepared sheet pan. Repeat with the remaining strips of dough, spacing the buns evenly on the pan. (At this point, the rolls can be wrapped securely in plastic wrap and stored in the refrigerator for up to 2 days or in the freezer for up to 1 month; when ready to bake, thaw and continue.) Cover the rolls loosely with a piece of lightly buttered plastic wrap and let them rest in a warm spot until puffy and nearly doubled in size, 1 to 1½ hours.

8. Preheat the oven to 350°F (180°C).

9. Brush the tops of the rolls with the egg wash, then sprinkle them with the sugar. Bake until golden brown but still moist, 18 to 20 minutes. Serve the rolls while still warm, preferably with coffee or hot chocolate.

TINY TIPS: *If you can't find cardamom seeds, buy green cardamom pods, split them open, and grind the seeds in a spice grinder or with a mortar and pestle; think coarse enough to speckle the dough but not so coarse that you chip a tooth (you'll have plenty of opportunity to do that playing ice hockey later). If all you have is ground cardamom, use a little more, as it's less intense than freshly ground.*

If you want to be super Scandinavian, source Swedish pearl sugar at your local specialty grocer, kitchen shop, or online and sprinkle it on top of the rolls in place of the granulated sugar.

Orange–Earl Grey Cream Scones

MAKES 8

Don't waste all that precious zest when you make the Winter Citrus Salad (page 195); use it for these light and flaky cream scones. Use fresh, high-quality Earl Grey tea, and if the tea leaves seem large, grind them in a spice grinder or crush them between your fingers. If there's zest to spare, stir 2 teaspoons and a splash of orange blossom honey into a stick of softened butter, and serve with the scones.

¾ cup (180 ml) heavy cream, plus more as needed and for brushing

1 teaspoon pure vanilla extract

2 cups (250 g) all-purpose flour, plus more for dusting

¼ cup (50 g) sugar

3 tablespoons loose Earl Grey tea leaves

2 teaspoons baking powder

½ teaspoon baking soda

½ teaspoon kosher salt

1 tablespoon grated orange zest

½ cup (1 stick/115 g) cold unsalted butter, cut into cubes (see Tiny Tip)

1. Line a rimmed half sheet pan with parchment paper.

2. Stir together the cream and vanilla in a small bowl or spouted glass measuring cup. Stir together the flour, sugar, tea, baking powder, baking soda, and salt in a large bowl. Mix in the orange zest with your fingers, rubbing it to help release its oils. Add the butter and work it into the flour mixture with your hands (pretend you're snapping your fingers together) until coarse crumbs form. Pour the cream mixture over the flour mixture and work it in with your hands or a fork until a shaggy dough forms. If the dough seems too dry, add another tablespoon or two of cream.

3. Turn the dough out onto a lightly floured surface and press it into a 6-inch (15 cm) disc. Cut the dough into quarters with a pastry scraper or sharp knife, then cut each quarter in half to create eight triangles. Place the scones on the prepared sheet pan, giving them room to spread, and chill them in the refrigerator while the oven preheats, about 15 minutes. (Or, freeze them until solid, put them in an airtight container, and freeze for a rainy scone day.)

4. Preheat the oven to 400°F (200°C).

5. Brush the tops of the scones with cream and bake until golden brown, 18 to 20 minutes. Ideally, serve them warm, although they will keep in an airtight container at room temperature for up to 3 days.

TINY TIP: *If your butter is frozen, just grate it with a box grater and carry on.*

Until We Hibernate Again

When the temperature warms up and it's finally time to pack up the cookie cutters and coats, shelve the boots, dust off the picnic basket, and (possibly) recalibrate our relationship with butter, we're always hoping that *just maybe* we'll get one more snow day—because when the weather is the worst, life at home is undeniably the best. Snowy days demand making your own entertainment, which for us means enticing everyone and anyone into the kitchen. Centering the day around a brisk outdoor activity followed by whatever wonder emerges from the oven is a delight we're reluctant to relinquish. We love the season's invitation to do nothing more than spend the weekend wondering how to make ourselves and the people we love cozy, whether that's by striking up the fire in the afternoon or mixing up cocktails all evening, baking or braising, constructing a trifle or tucking gifts under the tree, opening holiday cards or playing cards. Each winter day seems to amount to however many small joys we can pack into it. That's our kind of fun.

It was a great day when just the two of us (and one two-toothed recipe tester) sat by the roaring fire in Oregon's historic Timberline Lodge and toasted this project with frosty copper mugs of Moscow mules, a still-warm soft pretzel, crispy coins of kielbasa, and oozy fondue (all of which, not coincidentally, you'll have found in these pages). We hope that in this cookbook, you've found plenty of ways to provision yourself and your friends, whether you're staying in a snowy cabin or hunkering down at home. If not, get cracking! The snow will melt, and the window for winter indulgence is always a little shorter than it seems at the onset. We wish you the coziest of winters, and even more than that, we wish you the kind of restfulness that sets you up for an exciting year.

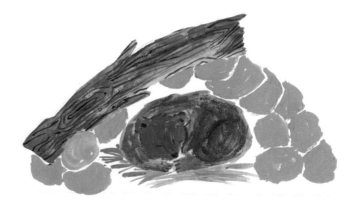

Pantry Provisions

Fantastic Food and Drink

Bobbie's Boat Sauce
bobbiesboatsauce.com
Step aside, sriracha; this is the new one-and-only condiment you'll ever need.

Bob's Red Mill
bobsredmill.com
Organic whole-grain flour power; produced in delicious Portland, Oregon.

Clear Creek Distillery
clearcreekdistillery.com
Fine Pacific Northwest fruit-based spirits, including the indispensable signature pear brandy.

Ferguson Farm
fergusonmaple.com
Maple syrup any way you like it, be that by the jug, or a wee tin resembling a log cabin.

Rancho Gordo
ranchogordo.com
Stock the pantry with eye-catching heirloom beans to instantly up your chili game.

Soma Chocolatemaker
somachocolate.com
From bean to bar to your ski house's secret chocolate stash.

The Spice & Tea Exchange
spiceandtea.com
Look for lavender for your nightcap, cardamom for your rolls, and tea for your toddies.

Steven Smith Teamaker
smithtea.com
The tastiest of teas for fireside sipping; plus, their matcha is matchless.

Stone Barn Brandyworks
stonebarnbrandyworks.com
Beautiful European-style fruit brandy and liqueurs made with Pacific Northwest bounty.

Thrive Market
thrivemarket.com
Swiftly stock snacks for every dietary persuasion.

Voilà
voila.coffee
Impeccably sourced handcrafted instant coffee—brownie booster, mousse magnifier, and because you just woke up but everyone's ski lessons start in ten minutes.

Aebleskiver Pans, Raclette Sets, and More

Filson
filson.com
Plush wool blankets, brrr-banishing apparel, and just the right dry bag for your new ice fishing habit.

Finex
finexusa.com
The finest in cast iron. Come for the fetching octagonal shape; stay for the pancakes.

FORLIFE
forlifedesign.com
Not only will the Stump teapot become one of your trustiest sidekicks (we even travel with one), it's available in ten comely colors.

Great Jones
greatjonesgoods.com
Sheet-pan stans, prepare to worship the Holy Sheet.

JK Adams
jkadams.com
Vermont-made heirloom-quality carving boards and cutting boards.

Le Creuset
lecreuset.com
The hardiest and handsomest of winter warmers, from cocottes to cast-iron Dutch ovens destined to be family heirlooms.

Lodge Cast Iron
lodgemfg.com
Iconic, will-have-it-forever USA-made cast-iron Dutch ovens, skillets, griddles, and muffin pans.

Nordic Ware
nordicware.com
Must-have winter- and holiday-themed pancake pans, made in Minneapolis.

Patagonia Provisions
patagoniaprovisions.com
Eco-friendly howlers, growlers, mugs, and more.

Scanpan
scanpan.com
Denmark-based makers of the most perfect nonstick 9-well aebleskiver pan in all the land.

Swissmar Raclette
swissmar.com
Just the place to get the perfect raclette set (may we recommend the red?).

Target
target.com
All the essentials, from oh-so-cute cabinware to Flexible Flyers.

Weber's Smokey Joe
weber.com
Have petite portable grill, will travel.

Acknowledgments

A hearty "Skål!" to illustrator Monica Dorazewski, whose scrumptious work brings whimsy and wonder to (almost) every page of this book.

No one balances our four-person chairlift quite like our dear editor, Judy Pray; working with her is like rolling the perfect snowperson base in one try, catching big air on a snow tube run, and landing a triple lutz all in one.

Being a part of the Artisan Books family means we've definitely won gold in the publishing company championships, and we applaud the incredibly talented team of designer Renata De Oliveira, design manager Jane Treuhaft, art director Suet Chong, and associate publisher Allison McGeehon, as well as the highest peak of publishers, Lia Ronnen.

Many thanks to copy editor Ivy McFadden, production editor Sibylle Kazeroid, and production manager Hanh Le for always making sure our pages are as pristine as fresh powder. We'd happily share a shotski at the Sawtooth Club with our peerless publicist, Theresa Collier, and assistant editor Bella Lemos. And our dynamic duo of agents, Sharon Bowers and Stacey Glick, always keep us on track, bobsled or no bobsled.

Always ready to provide feedback on all eighteen versions of the Salted Honey Butter Buns and solemnly evaluate the proper Cauliflower Nachos serving size ("The entire pan, right?") are our supportive and imperturbable—even in the face of some truly mind-blowing kitchen sink pileups—significant others, Jeff and Jamie. And a Banana Tarte Tatin–size thank-you to Bob, Pam, and Patricia, the world's best neighbors, for all the insightful tasting notes, beautiful test-kitchen-brightening bouquets, and fantastically fresh green-thumb-grown garden goodness.

You couldn't ask for a more charming trio of cooking companions, taste testers, and snow (-cone-loving) bunnies than the Peach, Cal-Bear, and Dash, who never hesitate to jump into the recipe development process (particularly any involving hot cocoa) with both feet and all the sticky fingers.

A round of Boozy Orange Bourbon Eggnog for Jen's family, whose childhood winter weekends at Dodge Ridge instilled both a healthy fear of any sort of snow sport and a profound love of staying behind at the cabin to tinker in the kitchen, and for Marnie's family, whose early years in the Midwest imbued a commitment to breaking out the full-family toboggan no matter the pitch of the slope, skiing until the last chair, and forever trying to match the outrageous coziness of her own childhood home.

Index